Charles de Gaulle's Legacy of Ideas

Charles de Gaulle's Legacy of Ideas

Edited by
Benjamin M. Rowland

LEXINGTON BOOKS
Lanham • Boulder • New York • Toronto • Plymouth, UK

Published by Lexington Books
A wholly owned subsidiary of The Rowman & Littlefield Publishing Group, Inc.
4501 Forbes Boulevard, Suite 200, Lanham, Maryland 20706
www.lexingtonbooks.com

Estover Road, Plymouth PL6 7PY, United Kingdom

British Library Cataloguing in Publication Information Available

Library of Congress Cataloging-in-Publication Data

Charles de Gaulle's legacy of ideas / [edited by] Benjamin M. Rowland.
    p. cm.
Includes bibliographical references.
ISBN 978-0-7391-6452-5 (cloth : alk. paper) — ISBN 978-0-7391-6454-9 (ebook)
    1. Gaulle, Charles de, 1890–1970—Political and social views. 2. France—Politics
and government—1958–1969. 3. France—Foreign relations—1958–1969. 4. France—
Economic policy—1945– 5. Political leadership—France—Case studies. I. Rowland,
Benjamin M.
    DC420.C456 2011
    944.083'6092—dc23   2011018752

∞™ The paper used in this publication meets the minimum requirements of American
National Standard for Information Sciences—Permanence of Paper for Printed Library
Materials, ANSI/NISO Z39.48-1992.

Printed in the United States of America

Contents

Preface

The essays collected in this book were written for a conference held in November 2009, "Charles de Gaulle's Legacy of Ideas," conducted by the European Studies program of the Johns Hopkins Nitze School of Advanced International Studies (SAIS) and sponsored by the Washington Foundation for European Studies.

De Gaulle has grown more and more appreciated over the years. His existential qualities—his courage, panache, and wit—make him an irresistible subject. Our writers are perhaps more inclined to celebrate his wisdom. In the great arguments of his career, de Gaulle's antagonists, figures like Churchill and Roosevelt, were often themselves great existential heroes. But in many respects de Gaulle's vision of the future often seems more prescient and balanced. In any event, it is this dimension of his legacy that our essays explore.

The volume is dedicated to Patrick McCarthy—a gifted teacher and colleague at the Johns Hopkins Bologna Center. McCarthy was a well-known student of the literature of modern French and Italian Politics. He wrote notable books on Celine and Camus as well as several studies of French and Italian political economy and language. He is remembered warmly for his taste, irony, and capacity for moral outrage. He died a few years ago, after a long and heroic struggle with Parkinson's disease. While he was by no means an uncritical admirer of the General, a volume on de Gaulle in honor of McCarthy is a combination that I suspect the Professor would have appreciated, as probably would the General, as well.

All our authors were friends of McCarthy's. And with the exception of Stuermer and myself, all are graduates from the European Studies doctoral program at SAIS. McCarthy was a genial animator of that program and

Stuermer has assisted it on numerous occasions. I myself have had the honor and pleasure to preside over it since its founding in 1970. The dissertations cover a wide range of subjects and are often interdisciplinary in their analysis—in a fashion reflecting McCarthy and Stuermer as well as my own writings. The program remains small and personal. Patrick would have been pleased to be the occasion for displaying some of its talents.

Acknowledgments

We thank Nancy Tobin for her help in organizing the November 2009 conference, "Charles de Gaulle's Legacy of Ideas," from which most of the articles are taken. We also thank Greg Fuller, who helped format the articles and put them in file-ready form.

Introduction

France, like any country, is in great part a product of its history—its defeats and victories, its great writers and thinkers, its statesmen and warriors.[1] Charles de Gaulle's absorption with French history always included a keen sense of his own place in it, including a conviction during World War II and perhaps beyond that he was France incarnate. The essays in this volume examine certain of the policies and positions de Gaulle pursued nationally and in the international arena, giving consideration to their significance in their own time, and today. Not everything de Gaulle did withstands the test of time. Nor, clearly, was everything beyond criticism in his own time. Nonetheless, a main finding, in the words of one essayist, is that de Gaulle, had an "uncanny sense of where history was going" and a skill to position his country accordingly. De Gaulle also stands as a testament to the power of individuals in history, a somewhat unfashionable point of view in modern university curriculums. Today, when France's destiny appears increasingly to depend on institutions beyond its national control, including a Europe badly wounded by a sovereign debt crisis and a global economic system accountable to no one, it seems timely to reconsider the record of the 20th century's greatest Frenchman and his skill at dealing with problems that surely appeared as intractable in his own time as do the problems besetting France today.

De Gaulle's vision of the French state was partly mystical, always calculated. Defining France's identity, de Gaulle insisted when he was in power, was a task that he alone could do. The alternative would have been to consign France's future to the *hoi polloi* of interest groups and partisan politics which were by definition incapable of looking after any interest except their own. De Gaulle also excelled in the tactics and minutiae of politics, for example, finding the *mot juste* and delivering it at the right moment. In the words of one de Gaulle scholar, "Beyond doubt his greatest achievement of all was to have succeeded, through the matchless use of language by which he could turn the prosaic into the heroic, in convincing his fellow citizens that what was often no more than unavoidable necessity was actually the brilliant triumph of will and ability."[2]

De Gaulle's national and international goals were intertwined. France's international stature was a wellspring for nourishing its national self regard— its appetite for *grandeur*—while at the same time diverting national attention from the pains of adjusting to the postwar world. Our essayist on Franco–German relations, Michael Stuermer, observes that whereas Germany saw the EEC as the means for escaping as much as possible from the nation-state, France's approach was just the opposite, seeing in the EEC a kind of "force multiplier" for the nation-state.

Each of the essays in this book looks at an area where de Gaulle had a strong view, as often as not in conflict with the conventional wisdom of his time. The opening essay, "De Gaulle's Visions for Europe" by David Calleo, examines de Gaulle's project for a confederal *"Europe d'etats"*, a structure intended to strengthen Europe, contain Germany, and keep the superpowers at a distance, without diminishing the political and economic sovereignty of its member states, France's in particular.

Two following essays examine aspects of de Gaulle's economic policy: "De Gaulle and the Dollar," by Christopher Chivvis, an exploration of de Gaulle's ideas for a return to the gold standard and "Gaullist Economic Policies: the Role of Indicative Planning," by Benjamin Rowland. Postwar France turned to indicative planning initially to manage and direct scarce capital resources to the task of rebuilding the country's infrastructure. De Gaulle's later support for indicative planning as an "ardent obligation" of the State eventually included many other economic sectors as well as social policies of participation and inclusion.

De Gaulle's support for planning did not prevent him from also advocating what at first glance seemed planning's intellectual opposite—a domestic economy increasingly open to liberal international competition and a monetary policy based on the gold standard. Advocacy of a gold standard was probably first and foremost a tactic by de Gaulle to challenge the reserve currency status of the dollar, a status that allowed the United States to project power internationally, exempt from the economic checks and balances that restrained the ambitions of other states. But de Gaulle's gold standard also had deeper moral and philosophical underpinnings. In his version, the State continued to have an important regulatory role. It also remained the ultimate guarantor of property rights, without which markets of any kind could not function. Indeed the juxtaposition of planning and a gold standard, the former an offspring of socialism or worse, and the latter the ultimate instrument of a liberal economy, suggests at a minimum that doctrinal consistency was for de Gaulle a distant second in importance to the perceived interests of the French State.

Foreign policy, as noted above, played a special role in de Gaulle's concept of the State. It provided a unifying focus for fractious national interests and a fountainhead for French *grandeur* and exceptionalism. In "Germany and the General," Michael Stuermer reflects that without Germany, de Gaulle might have ended his days "spending a quiet and boring pensioner's life." Instead, Germany both inspired and challenged de Gaulle in the realm of strategy during the interwar years, while after the war the Franco-German relationship and its special requirements defined the core of overall French diplomacy. Turning from France's most important bilateral relationship to a more marginal one, Thomas Row's "De Gaulle and the Italians" underscores De Gaulle's contempt for Mussolini's pretensions to make Italy a first-rate power at France's expense. With postwar reconciliation and the restoration, in his view, of the proper rank order between the countries, de Gaulle did not concern himself much with the affairs of France's "latin sister."

Finding space for France to play the independent world role de Gaulle desired gave rise to frequent differences and occasional confrontations with the superpowers, in particular the United States. An overview of Franco-U.S. relations is provided in Dana Allin's, "De Gaulle and American Power." There was not room enough in a bipolar world for France to realize its ambitions. Bipolarity or even worse, the United States as the world's sole "hyper power" called forth a structure of power where hubris and corruption were unavoidable.

One direct path to dismantling the superpower duopoly was to recognize China. As Lanxin Xiang writes in "De Gaulle and the 'Eternal China,'" from today's vantage point, French recognition of China, anticipating the United States by some six years was nothing if not prescient. At the time, however, it felt to the United States like a betrayal of numerous interests, not least in Vietnam. In "The Road to Phnom Penh: de Gaulle, the Americans, and Vietnam, 1944–1966," John Harper sorts through a multiplicity of motives that may have guided de Gaulle in his choice of policies. De Gaulle saw the U.S. character as "Carthaginian, not Roman," that is, merchants rather than warriors. He was thus persuaded that in the final analysis, the United States would avoid an escalation of hostilities that included a direct confrontation with China. Without such a confrontation, however, the U.S. position was unwinnable, making an eventual withdrawal the only alternative. Finally, in

"De Gaulle and the Middle East," Timo Behr analyzes de Gaulle's motives in publicly upbraiding Israel, a French client state during the Fourth Republic, in the aftermath of the Six Day War in 1967. De Gaulle predicted that by seizing territory beyond the 1949 boundaries, Israel would find itself in permanent conflict with neighboring Arab states and Palestine.

Was de Gaulle as truly rooted in French history and culture as he himself thought or was he an historical "parenthesis," still the greatest Frenchman of the twentieth century but, like Napoleon in the nineteenth, standing not as the principal shaper of events to come, but as a towering figure on a path his country did not or could not follow. None of his ability to manipulate current affairs or his sensitivity for the past necessarily guarantees de Gaulle a legacy. The essays in this collection, however, suggest that his reputation is intact and his legacy well earned.

Benjamin M. Rowland
February, 2011

NOTES

1. Asked to rank categories of men in the order of his admiration for them, de Gaulle answered: "first, great writers; next, great thinkers; third, great statesmen; and fourth, great generals." Charles Wilson, *The Last Great Frenchman* (New York: J. Wiley & Sons, 1993), p. 337.

2. Serge Berstein, *The Republic of de Gaulle, 1958–1969* (Cambridge: Cambridge University Press, 1993), p. 245.

Chapter 1

De Gaulle's Visions for Europe

David P. Calleo

The twentieth century saw a disturbing abundance of heroes—men of iron will who managed to impose themselves on history. Not all of them were benefactors of mankind. Some were plainly evil, such as Stalin, Mao or Hitler, who brought great suffering to their own people and often to the rest of the world. Even the good—the Wilsons, Churchills and Roosevelts—seem often flawed. They faced great challenges with courage and skill, but to later historians, their decisions sometimes seem questionable or downright wrong-headed.

In this exalted company, de Gaulle seems so far to stand up rather well. Not only did he play a weak hand with exhilarating panache but, from our present perspective, he seems to have put his country on the right side of history. France, which paid a terrible price for victory in the First World War, rebounded strongly after defeat in the Second. Arguably, France has been the leading European power throughout the second half of the twentieth century and is today probably better positioned to face the trials of this new century than any other major Western power, with the possible exception of Germany. De Gaulle most certainly deserves some of the credit.

Like most great leaders, de Gaulle had well-developed Machiavellian talents. But he also was inspired and disciplined by an uncanny sense of where history was going and the courage and agility to position his country to avoid the dangers and reap the benefits. While his leadership was inspirational, his goals were balanced, reasonable, and thus sustainable. De Gaulle's own view of history taught him not only how pusillanimous leaders allowed their countries to drift into disaster, but how gifted leaders were often done in by overreaching themselves. The successful hero required a vision and audacity but also *mesure*. This Gaullist combination of foresight, agility and balance

1

seems amply demonstrated in the foreign policy he established for the Fifth Republic in its evolving relations with the United States, Britain, Germany and Russia. Initially, he held strongly negative views toward all four. These derived from his lonely struggle to defend defeated France's long-term interests during World War II. In the postwar years, however, de Gaulle managed to manage relations with each to France's advantage.

De Gaulle's views toward the United States were heavily influenced by his wartime quarrel with Roosevelt. This was based on what de Gaulle saw as the President's lack of interest in France's postwar revival as a great power. Roosevelt, as de Gaulle perceived him, was illustrating the usual ambitions of a great power on the rise. The President eagerly welcomed the great role that America was poised to play during the postwar era. Idealism cloaked his will to power. But Roosevelt, unlike his Cold War successors who were to bind the United States to NATO, was leery of territorial commitments. Instead he saw the United States as a maritime power relying on its navy and giant economy to bring prosperous order to the world. As Roosevelt read the history of his times, Europe's pretensions and quarrels had given the world endless trouble. He looked forward to when his Pax Americana would end Europe's ceaseless warring and colonial oppression. Accordingly, the last thing Roosevelt wanted from the defeat of Germany and Japan was a revival of British and French imperial power. Instead, new states of native peoples would arise out of the imperial wreckage. The United States would be the patron of these new states.

De Gaulle warned Roosevelt that America could not manage the world alone. "It is the West," he told the President,

> that must be restored. If it regains its balance, the rest of the world, whether it wishes to or not, will take it for an example. If it declines, barbarism will ultimately sweep everything away. Now, Western Europe, despite its dissensions and its distress, is essential to the West. Nothing can replace the value, the power, the shining examples of these ancient peoples. (Unity, 270)

Roosevelt has sometimes been accused of having more sympathy for Stalin's Russia than for his own Western allies. Stalin and Roosevelt shared a disdain for de Gaulle's aspirations for France. Stalin refused France a seat among the victors at Yalta. De Gaulle, in turn, refused to recognize the Soviet-backed Lublin Poles. In effect, he was refusing to countenance the Soviet seizure of power in Eastern Europe. At heart, de Gaulle detested the Soviet totalitarian regime and saw Stalin as a barbarian chieftain threatening to overrun a quarreling Europe. To some extent, de Gaulle's relations with Russia were affected by his relations with France's own large communist party. Unlike many other elements of the old Third Republic, the communists had been major allies of the Gaullist resistance movement. In his brief stint as president of the new Fourth Republic, de Gaulle had brought the communists into the provisional government. But once de Gaulle had quit the Presidency of the Fourth Republic, he relied heavily on anti-communist themes as he began a massive new popular campaign for constitutional reform.

In opposing Roosevelt and Stalin during the war, de Gaulle's only real ally had been Churchill. But the alliance was only intermittent and relations between the two were often stormy. As de Gaulle saw it, Britain had chosen to be America's special Anglo-Saxon relation rather than to join France in leading the revival of Europe. Churchill, by choosing to appease Roosevelt, was betraying Britain's own interests as well as her European responsibilities.

De Gaulle's experience with the prewar Third Republic had convinced him that France could not succeed in holding its own in the world without a much stronger government. He was bitterly disappointed when the new Fourth Republic appeared largely as a copy of the Third. He resigned the Presidency when his populist campaign for constitutional reform had failed and retired to Colombey les Deux Eglises to write his wartime *Memoirs*. These emerged as a powerful manifesto spelling out his view of the wartime quarrels—including his opposition to Roosevelt's soaring global visions, Stalin's brutal and corrupt barbarism, and Churchill's betrayal of Europe. The *Memoirs* appeared just as the Algerian War was about to catapult de Gaulle into power, with a mandate for the radical constitutional reform he had been calling for since the 1930s.

By the time de Gaulle was back in power, however, his case for French constitutional reform was challenged by the swelling support for European integration. To the "Good Europeans" of the day, de Gaulle's vision of a strong French presidency seemed anachronistic in comparison with the European vision embodied in the nascent institutions of European economic integration. Although de Gaulle had appointed Jean Monnet to head the French Plan at the start of the Fourth Republic, he had not supported Monnet's Coal and Steel Community of 1950. As he was coming in to power in 1958, he also seemed unenthusiastic at the prospect of French membership in the European Economic Community and Euratom.

De Gaulle was leery of the Monnet institutions not because he opposed large-scale European economic planning. His objection was to the accompanying federalist superstructure. Monnet's followers and those of the European Commission's first president, Walter Hallstein, were inspired by the widespread expectation among the federalists that economic integration would "spill over" into political integration. While scornfully rejecting Monnet's political faith, de Gaulle recognized the practical value of his economic projects. De Gaulle could accept, and indeed strongly support, the institutions of European economic integration, even including the politically ambitious Commission. Support for economic integration was not a new sentiment for de Gaulle. At the time of the Marshall plan, he had gone out of his way to praise the *"très vaste portée"* of the American proposals. Not only did they promise serious aid for Europe's rebuilding, but they also pressed European states to harmonize a general economic plan—*"une initiative clairvoyante et dont on peux espérer qu'elle sera féconde, precisement parce qu'elle engage l'Europe à la solidarité."*

In trying to understand these apparent tensions in de Gaulle's views on European economic integration, it is worth remembering that while de Gaulle was steeped in the traditional French faith in the state and appreciation for expert bureaucracies, he was also a firm believer in the gold standard, precisely because of the fiscal and monetary balance it required. Here he was encouraged by his economic adviser, the philosopher-economist Jacques Rueff, who well exemplified the special character of French Liberalism. Alongside the traditional Liberal faith in the market Rueff also accepted the need for a competent and active state. Such states were needed to uphold the regulations that would make a free market possible. But such states also needed to bind themselves to international rules, like the gold standard, that required measured fiscal and monetary policies and a respect for the rights of other states. By the mid 1960s, de Gaulle and Rueff would invoke this French-style Liberalism to attack the U.S. dollar's role as a reserve currency—the role sanctioned by a "gold-exchange standard" that compelled others to sustain America's increasingly abandoned fiscal and monetary policies during the Vietnam War and thereafter.

By the 1970s Gaullist monetary Liberalism was beginning to provide common ground for French and German opposition to American manipulation of the dollar. By the 1990s, this affinity blossomed into the Franco-German project of the euro. This was a remarkable evolution from the early postwar era, when France, fighting major colonial wars in Indochina and then Algeria, had lurched from one currency crisis to another. But after several years of Gaullist *mesure* prospects were radically improved for a French-German European partnership rooted in a consensus for fiscal and monetary discipline.

While de Gaulle was early on drawn to the possibilities for economic integration, he continued to oppose political integration that meant a surrender of sovereignty to European institutions. On the other hand, he strongly believed in the need for political coordination among the member states of Europe. His solution had emerged in the Fouchet Plan, at first rejected by the Six but soon gradually adopted, de facto, as European states felt the need for political cooperation after the oil shocks. As de Gaulle had insisted, however, each state was to retain a veto in matters deemed of vital national interest—the principle laid down in the "Empty Chair" crisis which refused the Hallstein Commission's bid for genuine supranational power. In practice this worked well enough while the EEC's membership and scope remained relatively limited.

Whatever de Gaulle's ambivalence about economic federalism, he remained unambiguously opposed to political and military federalism. Before he came to power in 1958, his most bitter opposition had been to the European Defense Community, proposed in 1952 by the French Prime Minister, René Pleven. Indeed, de Gaulle emerged briefly from retirement to ensure the project's defeat in the French National Assembly of 1954. The EDC issue provoked him to state clearly his opposition to European integration based upon a loss of sovereignty for Europe's nation-states.

In de Gaulle's view, however, the principal threat to sovereignty in the military sphere came not from Europeanist ambitions themselves, but from their linkage to NATO and the Americans. While de Gaulle obviously understood the critical importance of the American commitment to defend Europe against the Soviets, he nevertheless vigorously opposed arrangements in NATO that separated France's military from French sovereignty. Once in power, he effectively separated French forces from American control and, in due course, expelled NATO forces from France entirely. These moves reflected a series of major issues that de Gaulle faced at the time: How would the recently rebellious French military be reformed after Algeria? What was the proper strategy for Europe's defense or for a nuclear-armed France's own national defense?

After Algeria, de Gaulle sought to reorient the French military from colonial warfare to nuclear deterrence. He pursued France's nuclear capabilities—already a priority for the Fourth Republic. He was concerned not to accept American assistance if it meant the loss of France's independent capabilities. De Gaulle's emphasis on nuclear deterrence put him at odds with the Kennedy Administration's new "flexible response" strategy for NATO—in effect an effort to emphasize conventional defense over nuclear deterrence. This reflected American apprehensions over the advances in Soviet nuclear capabilities. After Sputnik, the United States began to seem vulnerable to direct nuclear attack from Soviet intercontinental weapons. American strategic planners were understandably unenthusiastic at former plans that counted on rapid escalation to an intercontinental response in the event of a Soviet attack in Europe. By contrast, French strategic doctrine (and British) justified Europe's national deterrents as triggers to ensure that any war in Europe would soon escalate into a full-scale transatlantic nuclear war. At all costs,

European strategic planners hoped to avoid a war between the superpowers limited to European territory. Accordingly, American insistence on "flexible response," meaning a more credible conventional deterrence in Europe, was one of the principal reasons for France's formal withdrawal from NATO. Expelling NATO bases from French territory made the notion of conventional deterrence for Europe highly problematic.

America's growing diffidence at using its intercontinental nuclear deterrent for Europe's defense suggested the need for a collective European response. Before de Gaulle returned to power, the Fourth Republic had been exploring the possibility of sharing the development of nuclear weapons with Italy and Germany—speculative exercises that the incoming Gaullist regime quickly terminated. Thereafter, de Gaulle resisted firmly initiatives to transform the French deterrent into a deterrent for Europe as a whole. France's deterrent would remain strictly national. Indeed, right to the end of the Cold War, French military plans apparently called for using French tactical nuclear weapons to stop Soviet forces from advancing through Germany. Needless to say such plans were not popular in Germany and did little to advance Franco-German cooperation in the military sphere. In effect, de Gaulle was caught in the contradiction between enthusiasm for an independent Europe maneuvering between the two blocs and his firm unwillingness to share French nuclear assets with his European partners. De Gaulle developed European military debates in a fashion that allowed him to avoid the real issue. In his opposition to the EDC, for example, he focused on its fundamentally Atlanticist and bureaucratic character while ignoring the implications for solidarity among West European states. In effect, he was an Atlanticist for the rest of Europe—relying on America's deterrent—and a nationalist for France—using the *force de dissuasion* for purely national insurance.

Military issues in de Gaulle's presidency were intimately connected with his views about how Germany was to be reintegrated into the European system. At the outset, his outlook on this subject was highly traditional. Indeed, his early postwar views would have been familiar to Cardinal Richelieu. A divided Germany had, he argued, many advantages for both the Germans and their neighbors. If the Germans themselves wished it, Germany might ultimately be united in some federal construction, but not with a centralized Reich as its government. In the early 1950s, de Gaulle was not at all in favor of German rearmament. This was a development, he said, that France could not permit. As we have seen, the Fourth Republic proposed a European Defence Community, a device for Germany to rearm but without creating a national German army. De Gaulle refused to support it. France would not sacrifice her own independent military to prevent German rearmament. In the end the French were compelled to see a German national army formed in close collaboration with the Americans in NATO.

To summarize thus far, before he resumed power in 1958, de Gaulle's speeches and writings, and above all his *Memoirs,* indicate that he had long been brooding over the big questions of France's own future. His vision indicated a deeper, if darker, sense of history than his more intellectually fashionable Europeanist contemporaries. Nevertheless, before he returned to power in 1958, his views might be considered fundamentally nationalist and provincial. He was preoccupied with restoring France's national psyche, deeply worried at the prospect of a German national revival and grudging toward proposals for European integration. His views were typical of a highly intelligent conservative nationalist. It is not surprising that his opponents dismissed him as an inconvenient anachronism. In the end, however, de Gaulle was more radical than his critics. He did not believe the age of superpowers would long endure, and he was not willing to concede Russia's new empire in Eastern Europe.

Returning to power in 1958 proved a great stimulus to his creative imagination. His first initiative was a proposal to Eisenhower and Macmillan for a tripartite concert to regulate global affairs. This idea was predictable, given his wartime experience, but also backward-looking. The tepid response from the old allies stimulated his imagination in a more European direction. In place of the geopolitical alliance he had once offered Churchill, de Gaulle turned to Germany.

The first sign of a new European enthusiasm came as de Gaulle ended the Algerian War and suppressed the Civil War that threatened to follow. In the process, France's remaining African empire was refashioned into a less colonial and more durable relationship. To wean his countrymen from their fading imperial glory, de Gaulle needed to offer a newer sort of national grandeur. Pursuing Europe, France could rejuvenate its economy and restore its tradition of technological prowess. Gaullist planning, with a return to fiscal and monetary discipline, could greatly strengthen the French economy. Accepting European competition and entering a European scale would allow French industry to be a global as well as a regional player.

The problem was how to gain Europe without losing France. Monnet's "spillover" model for Europe would undermine the French state and replace it with a weak federal system with no real popular support and hence easily dominated by American competition: To embrace Europe but reject Monnet, de Gaulle turned to a rival model for European integration the confederal "Europe of States" embodied in his Fouchet Plan. This was close to the interwar model for *Paneuropa* put forth in the 1920s by Count Coudenhove-Kalergi. Coudenhove, like de Gaulle, feared Europe's being dominated in a world of big external superpowers—Soviet Russia and capitalist America. To flourish and sustain their own identity and self-determination Coudenhove believed Europe's states would have to learn to cooperate in order to define and pursue their own general interests. The World War had indicated that Europe could not be united by conquest. Germany had failed as Napoleonic France had failed before her. Continuing attempts to unify Europe by internal conquest would grow more and more self-destructive and merely hasten the domination of outsiders.

Not surprisingly, World War II had not lessened the force of Coudenhove's arguments. Like de Gaulle, Coudenhove had not believed a federal Europe could or should aim to replace Europe's ancient nation-states. Only the old states had the populist legitimacy needed to sustain a strong and responsive government in the present highly challenging age. Coudenhove proposed a confederal Union not designed to rob its members of their sovereignty. Instead, old states in cooperating would greatly enhance their effectiveness and hence their own real sovereignty. In this process they would not lose their national identity, but would acquire an additional "European" identity, a sort of collective super-ego among Europe's national states.

Putting these ideas into effective practice required building collective institutions where Europe's states could seek to determine and coordinate common interests. Coudenhove's focus had been continental rather than Atlantic. He was skeptical of England's devotion to Europe. His hopes lay with France and Germany. United in a common European cause, they could remain world powers and avoid being demoted into playthings of the superpowers. De Gaulle had flirted with these ideas in his interwar writings and had sketched confederal proposals in his wartime speeches and *Memoirs*. He began to pursue these ideas in earnest with the Fouchet Plan.

The Fouchet Plan was, of course, not popular with the Monnet-Hallstein "Good Europeans," and hence with the European Commission which they dominated. To Monnet's followers, the "spillover" model still seemed plausible and infinitely preferable. De Gaulle's "Europe of States" would be a retrogression to a nationalist Europe. Nevertheless, at one point all six EEC states except the Netherlands agreed to adhere to the plan. The Dutch proved obdurate and the issue grew tangled with Britain's belated attempt to join the EEC, a move vetoed by de Gaulle. This led to great bitterness among the French, the British and the Americans, as well as among the Six themselves. De Gaulle withdrew his Fouchet proposal by 1962. Most of its provisions were later adopted as European states began pursuing more and more elaborate "political cooperation" since the oil shocks of the early 1970s. De Gaulle, meanwhile, concentrated on the French-German core. He quickly realized that the success of such arrangements depended primarily on the degree to which France and Germany could agree on European policies. There followed an intensive campaign to woo the Germans away from their strong Atlanticist predilections. De Gaulle toured Germany and Adenauer came to France and both countries witnessed heartwarming scenes of reconciliation between the two old enemies.

Germans were divided as old cultural splits reopened. German Catholics in the CDU and CSU tended to favor the French connection. CDU Protestants, the Liberal FDP and the secular Socialists shared greater reserve. Nevertheless, in the long run de Gaulle and Adenauer's grand reconciliation appears to have taken hold. To the present day, publics in both countries deeply favor an intimate relationship between the two nations and believe it is essential for welfare of each and of Europe as a whole. Governments have built close ties at all levels that continue to operate in favor of concerted action. Even when leaders are not in close agreement, or differences are sharp, a large part of the bureaucracy on both sides works to limit the damage. Building this close relationship has been a matter of several decades. Its success is a tribute to the skill of diplomats on both sides. Above all, it reflects certain broad shifts that brought French diplomacy in line with Germany's own vital interests. Critical among these was Germany's national reunification.

Like most other French leaders of his generation, De Gaulle had spoken out against reunification. But de Gaulle was too good a nationalist to imagine Germans remaining contented with their division. If France were basing her future on a European confederacy formed around a special relationship with Germany, France could not be seen as implacably hostile to Germany's reuniting. Even if the Catholic wings of the CDU/CSU were diffident about reunion with the Protestant East, when the opportunity presented itself, most probably nationalism would prevail. In any event, Germans would decide, and it was not in France's interest to be narrowly tied to any one view of Germany's future. Nor should France be tied to a West European confederacy that assumed a permanent division of Europe. Events in Germany probably encouraged de Gaulle to update his European visions. Adenauers's advanced age had made him vulnerable. His criticism of Kennedy for a weak reaction to the Berlin Wall, along with his continuing close friendship with France in the face of de Gaulle's veto of Britain, had weakened German–American relations. In due course, Adenauer was forced out and replaced by his Protestant CDU rival, Ludwig Erhard, a liberal economist who had strongly opposed Germany's joining the EEC in the first place. French–German relations deteriorated sharply.

Within a year, however, a "German Gaullist" cabal had forced Erhard out and Germany was ruled by a Great Coalition that included the Social Democrats (SPD). Their leader, Willy Brandt, former Mayor of West Berlin, had become

Foreign Minister. He was strongly inclined toward an *Ostpolitik* designed to open new connections with Russia and with the East European states. Brandt was careful not to challenge Soviet hegemony or to patently seek to undermine the communist economies. His aim was to restore human ties, while offering loans to purchase the consumer goods the Soviet system could not produce. Within three years a new election had brought Brandt to the chancellorship.

These abrupt shifts in Germany's governing coalitions posed a considerable challenge to French diplomacy. But de Gaulle had long anticipated this reawakened German interest, as early as 1959, with a bold innovation of his own—the concept of "Europe from the Atlantic to the Urals." In effect, de Gaulle began to propose the reunification of Europe. Implicit in his vision was the collapse of the Soviet empire together with Russia's abandoning of its communist regime. The idea was not so new for de Gaulle. He had always thought communism a detestable and hopelessly inefficient regime that would go away. Russia, however, would remain. Under communism, Russia had grown grotesquely overextended. The regime would implode, and it would be up to the rest of Europe to respond creatively—in a fashion that would preserve the peace and make the best of the new opportunities.

Europe, meanwhile, should resist a vision of détente where the two superpowers collaborated to preserve "stability" through arms control. This vision of détente would fail because the bipolar system of the Cold War had left both sides overextended—the Americans no less than the Soviets. Both had carved out roles for themselves that they could not sustain as the rest of the world continued to recover from the war. America's weakness was clear enough in the mounting problems of the dollar. De Gaulle's attack on America's dollar policy thus went hand in hand with his assault on the Soviet Union's overextended position in Eastern Europe. France's attack on the gold exchange standard was a warning that Europe would not continue to finance American deficits forever.

One final element was needed to complete de Gaulle's deconstruction of the bipolar order. This was his opening to China. This great Asian state, so brutally treated in the nineteenth and twentieth centuries, had been in the grip of a terrible reaction. But it would rejuvenate itself, de Gaulle asserted, and demand its place among the world's great states. China's rise would force Russia to disgorge its imperial spoils and, among other things, sweep away America's lingering pretension to global dominance.

All this had already come to pass in de Gaulle's imagination a half century ago. It looks remarkably close to the plural world that now confronts us. No doubt de Gaulle's policies were sometimes inconsistent. Nevertheless, he was remarkably prescient. He did his best to put France, Europe, and America on the right side of history. When presented with so elegant, courageous, and benevolent a hero, it seems churlish to complain about the details.

Chapter 2

De Gaulle and the Dollar

Christopher S. Chivvis

On February 4, 1965, French President Charles de Gaulle held a press conference in which he called for the abolition of the Bretton Woods international monetary system and a return to the classical gold standard. The Bretton Woods system, designed during World War II, had been in force since 1958. It was a novel design in international monetary history whereby all members' currencies were fixed to the U.S. dollar, which itself was fixed to gold at $35 dollars per ounce. The gold standard, by contrast, was considered by most leading economists to be a thing of the past "like oil lamps and sailing ships" as Raymond Aron quipped. John Maynard Keynes had delivered a major blow to the gold standard's reputation in his writings on the "fetish" of gold in the 1920s, and most post–World War II economists had followed Keynes's lead, arguing that the gold standard was an outmoded relic of the nineteenth century. To support the gold standard in the 1960s was to show the antediluvian nature of one's political and economic views. De Gaulle's call for a return to gold accordingly met with derision in most major world capitals, especially the United States, where U.S. Secretary of Treasury Henry Fowler remarked was "quite against the mainstream" thinking in international policy circles.

De Gaulle's effort to return the world system of payments to the gold standard would last two years. Ultimately, it would fail, and by 1967 France had given up in favor of closer cooperation with its European partners and a more conciliatory position vis-à-vis the United States. In the end, de Gaulle's policy may actually have done more to set French interests back than to help them. Had de Gaulle pursued a more moderate course, endorsing, for example, an international currency managed by the International Monetary Fund—an alternative proposal that was circulating and far more popular not only with the United States, but also with France's European partners—something more constructive might have been achieved. His adherence to the gold standard thus appeared to many to be only a tactical maneuver in his broader campaign for independence in foreign affairs. Examined closely, however, the policy reveals a deeper philosophical and political core that should still interest the world today.

If we are to understand the nature and philosophical significance of de Gaulle's call for a return to gold, it is thus essential to look beyond the narrow policy objectives of the moment and put the initiative in its proper historical context. By calling for a return to the gold standard, de Gaulle was clearly working to further a number of foreign policy goals, but his argument was also rooted in his deep political conservatism. The gold standard suited his political philosophy on aesthetic, logical, and moral levels. Here the views of the French liberal intellectual and political economist Jacques Rueff were particularly important. Rueff's exposition of the superior virtues of the gold standard fit not only the practical needs of Gaullist statecraft, but also the French President's general vision of how the international system ought to be organized. These views, and the conservative philosophy in which they were grounded, are the subject of this essay.

DE GAULLE'S GOLD POLICY

Debate over the world's monetary problems is normally relegated to economists. In part, this is on account of the often complex, technical nature of international monetary arrangements and also because such issues are quite dry and rarely seize the imagination of the broad public. Quite dry, at least, when discussed by most leaders. Less so, when the figure is Charles de Gaulle, who, on February 4, 1965, pronounced the virtues of the gold standard, demonstrating not only a unique talent for bringing out the aesthetic and moral dimension of economic issues, but also an impressive grasp of those problems' technical side. The latter particularly surprised many observers, who had long assumed that the seventy-four-year-old General had little interest or grasp of economics.

Speaking from his rostrum in the Elysée Palace, De Gaulle declared that an international monetary system in which the dollar was held as a reserve currency was inequitable and had become an unrecognized tool of American global power. Bretton Woods was thus "abusive and dangerous," because the dollar's reserve role in the system allowed the United States to "indebt itself freely to foreign countries," thereby permitting America both to appropriate foreign business and engage in far-reaching military operations around the world.

The dollar's special role in the system must end, he said. The only acceptable alternative was a return to the gold standard, whereby dollars had no real value and gold had a "nature that does not change." It was "held, eternally and universally, as the unalterable fiduciary value par excellence." For the United States to give away dollars in exchange for foreign currency was painless, he pointed out. Giving away gold "that is possessed only for having earned it" involved real "risks and sacrifice." In short, the gold standard, by replacing dollar reserves with an objective and neutral reserve, would check America's growing power in the world system. It would also stabilize the system, whose foundations were too dependent on the fortunes of the United States. The result would be better for all parties concerned.

To fully understand the meaning and significance of this argument, it is important to view it in its appropriate historical context. This context has several dimensions, political, military, and economic. Let us begin with a brief look at the political and military situation as it had developed in recent years.

THE DOLLAR AND THE DEFENSE OF EUROPE

The political and military problems of the 1960s are the subjects other essays in this volume. One or two brief points of relevance to de Gaulle's gold standard initiative, however, are worth emphasizing here. Western Europe's recovery from the Second World War had been remarkable by all measures—not least by comparison with post–Cold War cases of postconflict reconstruction. France, along with Germany, Italy, the Netherlands, and others reestablished their pre-war levels of income by the early 1950s, and then continued to experience high rates of growth throughout the next two decades, until the inflations of the 1970s hit. High rates of economic growth, along with a burgeoning mass-consumer culture, helped stabilize European societies, immunizing them against the revolutions of right and left that had shaken the world in the first half of the century. West European states thus grew more confident in their ability to protect themselves from the threat of Communism, domestic or foreign. The confidence of de Gaulle's foreign policies—like those of his younger contemporary Willy Brandt—was a reflection of Europe's return to a position of economic health and hence renewed influence in international affairs.

Europe's positive economic trend had two important consequences when it came to de Gaulle's gold policy. For one, it encouraged the view that the military protectorate that the United States had established in Europe was no longer necessary. There was, of course, by no means a consensus on the issue, but Europe's renewed confidence in its ability to manage its own affairs contributed to a sense that American troops were as much part of the problem as part of the solution. At the same time, Europe's rapid economic recovery encouraged, in the United States, the view that Europe ought to foot a larger part of its own defense bill. As U.S. military expenditure in other parts of the world grew, the pressure on Europe to share the burden also increased.

In the early 1960s, these two issues converged in debates about the international monetary system. In the early 1960s, confidence in the U.S. dollar was waning as a result of a U.S. balance of payments deficit, which led to speculation that the dollar would be devalued. Because the dollar's link to gold was the anchor of the whole Bretton Woods system, the fragility of the dollar was a problem not only for the United States, but for all the economies participating in the system. In part the U.S. deficit reflected U.S. government spending overseas, a large portion of which went to support U.S. troops stationed in Europe. It followed logically from this that the weakness of the dollar was the result of the U.S. inability to sustain its commitment to European defense. Those who saw that commitment as more of an imposition than an aid naturally argued that those troops should be drawn down. In the United States, by contrast, the situation was evidence that Europe itself, now recovered, ought to foot more of the bill for its own defense. Because the size of the U.S. deficit roughly equaled the cost of the U.S. forces stationed in the Federal Republic, the United States negotiated an offset agreement with the Adenauer government, whereby the now booming Germany would guarantee purchase of a set amount of U.S. goods to ensure that the U.S. dollar did not suffer from America's commitment to defense at the Fulda Gap.

These arrangements, and others like them, however, did little but bring temporary succor to the fragile dollar. The durability of Bretton Woods, as a result, was perpetually in doubt. This in turn, checked economic growth. There were, accordingly, various plans for reform of the system. Some involved ad hoc measures. Others involved the establishment of international reserve currencies. The most audacious, however, was the plan put forward by Jacques Rueff.

RUEFF'S MONETARY CONSERVATISM

For many years, Rueff had been pressing de Gaulle to carry out deep reform of not only the French monetary and financial system, but also Bretton Woods. One of the leading free market thinkers of twentieth-century Europe,

Rueff was also a man who served in the highest ranks of the French civil service during the interwar period, when Europe was convulsed by the political-economic fallout from the Great War. An engineer by training, he was also a man with a penchant for philosophy—the philosophy of the later nineteenth-century neo-positivists as well as that of Henri Bergson—and his combination of this philosophical bent with his engineer's perspective was always at the core of his reflections on the nature of modern economic life. That perspective shaped his interpretation of the interwar crisis of liberalism, drove his thinking in the postwar era, and ultimately lay behind his effort to convince de Gaulle that a return to the gold standard was imperative not only for France, but for Europe, and ultimately the United States.

Three experiences in particular shaped Rueff's thinking during the interwar years. First was the central European inflations of the 1920s, which Rueff later linked with the rise of authoritarian regimes in these regions. Second was the rise of the Popular Front in France, and the contemporaneous collapse of the *franc poincaré*, which had burdened France for several years during the depression. The third was the collapse of the gold standard in the early 1930s, which he blamed primarily on the British efforts to push the burdens of postwar adjustment off onto other countries—in particular France, which Rueff noted had followed a more prudent monetary and fiscal policy in the later 1920s. He saw a parallel between Britain's unwillingness to accept discipline in the 1920s and America's in the 1960s.

Together these experiences formed the basis for Rueff's wartime opus, *L'Ordre Social,* a work that has been too often ignored in the history of twentieth-century political and economic thought. Rueff's work, which can be read instructively alongside Hayek's much slimmer, *Road to Serfdom,* links the failure to restore monetary stability in the postwar era to the rise of totalitarianism in the 1930s and the concomitant crisis of liberalism. This is a view that many of Rueff's friends in the Mount Pelerin Society shared, although Rueff goes much further than Hayek or the Germans in elaborating the ways in which inflation erodes and corrupts the working of the liberal democratic order at its deepest levels.

Like the other members of the post–World War II free market movement, Rueff wrote forcefully in favor not only of the benefits of the price mechanism but also of against the rising chorus of voices who favored economic planning as a means of taming capitalism. Like them, he believed that the free market system of the nineteenth century, while not without its faults, had in general been beneficial to the European societies in which it was practiced. (In this, he was probably correct, although no doubt over-estimated the extent to which the liberal political economy had been the standard in nineteenth century Europe.)

It may seen difficult, on the surface, to square liberal views such as these with de Gaulle's Catholic conservatism. Politically and philosophically, de Gaulle had little in common with the liberals, although it is worth noting that liberals had often allied themselves with authoritarian figures in the nineteenth century when their interests were threatened, most notably under Napoleon III. Understanding what Rueff's philosophy offered that was of interest to de Gaulle requires understanding two fundamental, related aspects of Rueff's broad liberal vision, aspects on which he differed greatly from the majority of his liberal economic contemporaries—and, it is worth noting, their later twentieth-century progeny.

The first aspect of Rueff's thought that brought his views more closely into line with de Gaulle's was his inherent respect for the state. Unlike many members of the Mount Pelerin society, Rueff never shared the view that the state was problematic. To the contrary, his argument in *L'ordre social* was grounded in an essentially Hobbesian argument about the nature and necessity of the state for maintaining order in human society. Rueff had been trained at the elite *Ecole Polytechnique* for high-level civil servants and served the state throughout his formative years. From his perspective, the state was, at the most fundamental level, the guarantor of order, which was, in turn, a prerequisite for the free market—and hence individual freedom. Rueff noted that the free market was "nothing but a modest outgrowth" of the system of property rights, of which the state was the ultimate guarantor. Market mechanisms allowed for the relaxation of authoritarian systems of order, but the state remained, beneath the market, the ultimate guarantor of social order.

This fact leads to the second dimension of his thought in which he differed from many of his contemporary free market thinkers. For Rueff, not only did the functioning of the free market rest ultimately on the state, but the state also had a crucial role to play in ensuring the cultural and moral development of society. It was not enough to simply ensure the functioning of the price mechanism. The state also had a responsibility to develop the national civilization—investing in national defense, art, and culture, but also ensuring an acceptable distribution of national wealth. A society that was merely pacified, Rueff argued, would be morally deplorable. Servants of the state, in other words, would use the free market to increase prosperity and permit individual freedoms, but would also correct for the more perverse effects of the price mechanism.

It followed naturally from this proposition that the state had to protect property rights, but also had the right to interfere in their distribution, correcting as necessary for the deficiencies of the market. Rueff did not believe that the state should interfere with the market itself, only that it should engage to balance the effects of the market once the price mechanism had served its function. In other words, Rueff's liberalism was devoid of the libertarian and often antisocial dimension that is too often associated with the liberals of his day, a frame of mind that brought him closer to the Catholic conservatism of de Gaulle. (Rueff himself was a Jew converted to Catholicism early in his life.)

At the same time, however, Rueff held that the primary function of the state was to ensure the functioning of the price mechanism. This required monetary stability, and it thus followed that one of the state's fundamental responsibilities was to defend the stability of the monetary system. Throughout the 1920s and 1930s, Rueff had witnessed the malign effects of budget deficits on monetary stability and had seen the ways in which the accumulation of budget deficits in various countries could create international monetary instability, unleash a cycle of competitive devaluation and protectionism, undermining, Rueff believed, not only Europe's economic health but also its political unity. Budget deficits themselves, Rueff noted, were often the result of underlying disagreements in society, which the lacunae in national budgets papered over. The social conflict inherent in these deficits was then washed out into the monetary system, where its consequences were ultimately no less malign, only less well understood.

The upshot of this view was a very conservative position on monetary policy and a deep belief in the relationship between monetary and social stability and the importance of both to the flourishing of the national civilization. For Rueff, the gold standard was the time-tested means of maintaining monetary stability. All other monetary systems were too subject to political mismanagement and hence service to particular rather than general interests. In the context of the cold war and the threat of social discontent, Rueff believed, the gold standard offered the only durable basis on which to build French democracy, European integration, and closer transatlantic ties. This was the basic vision that underlay his multi-year effort to convince de Gaulle that a return to the gold standard had to be a priority if de Gaulle's reformist foreign policy were to be complete.

RUEFF AND DE GAULLE

There seems little doubt that de Gaulle was influenced by Rueff in his arguments for a return to gold. De Gaulle did not frequently lavish credit for his initiatives on others, and so there is thus no way to prove definitively that he was drawing directly on Rueff in his 1965 press conference. But all the evidence points in this direction. For one, several of Rueff's friends were members of de Gaulle's inner *coterie*. To be sure, the men who might advise de Gaulle formally on economic matters—the young future president and Gaullist Finance Minister Valery Giscard d'Estaing and his counterpart at the Banque de France, Wilfred Baumgartner, were both dedicated Keynesians who deplored Rueff's ideas and disparaged them at every possible opportunity. Indeed, in Baumgartner's case, the rivalry was personal, and rooted in the two men's professional competition in the Ministry of Finance in the 1930s—a competition in which Baumgartner ultimately prevailed. Nevertheless, despite the Keynesian perspective of many of the economic experts in de Gaulle's government, some of the key figures who held other no less important posts, were far more inclined toward Rueff's views. The most important of these men was surely Maurice Couve de Murville, who served as de Gaulle's Foreign Minister through most of the 1960s. Couve had been a protégé of Rueff's in the finance ministry in the 1930s, and the two men held each other in high esteem throughout their lives, meeting regularly in the postwar era to discuss the major issues of the day over drinks in Rueff's apartment on the Rue de Varennes. Couve makes clear in his memoirs his support for the gold policy, and Rueff also notes the fact that Couve was frequently ensuring that the President remained fully appraised of the international monetary problems of the early 1960s, and the arguments for a return to gold.

Moreover, Rueff himself had access to the President thanks to his key role in the 1958 reform of French finances that accompanied de Gaulle's return to power. De Gaulle had instigated that reform as the financial leg of his tripartite strategy for stabilizing a country that seemed on the brink of war. The other two legs—responding to the crisis in Algeria and constitutional reform—tend to receive greater attention in the historical literature, but de Gaulle's financial reforms were no less important, as the austerity measures set an important tone for the Gaullist republic, signaling a return to discipline and break with the more lax fiscal policies of the Fourth Republic—and its consequent monetary crises. De Gaulle's France would not tolerate the indignity of a franc that was on the brink of collapse and in need of rescue packages from the (U.S. dominated) International Monetary Fund. The Gaullist republic would be stable, and so would the franc. Indeed, if France was to revive, de Gaulle recognized the need for domestic financial reform, and, in 1958, chose Rueff over his own Finance Minister Antoine Pinay, to design the financial reforms on which the economic success of his new republic would rest. One product of the reforms, which were given de Gaulle's imprimatur in December 1958, was a new currency that some would come to call the *franc-Rueff*.

The Rueff reforms were, in general, successful, at least in bringing the French government's finances under control. They failed to end inflation in the long run, however, in large part on account of their partial application, itself a result of the animosity of Baumgartner and the Keynesians at the *Banque de France*. De Gaulle would hear Rueff on financial and monetary issues several times in subsequent years. Even when the President did not grant Rueff a hearing in person, he would accept Rueff's frequent memoranda on developing problems in the international monetary system. These visits and missives, which continued from 1958 through 1965 and beyond, cannot but have been at the root of de Gaulle's decision to pursue a return to the gold standard in 1965.

After all, there were few others in France or elsewhere who believed so strongly that a return to the gold standard was desirable, or even possible. The challenges to the French president's vision were indeed formidable. For one, the United States was averse to the idea, as the reaction of its Treasury secretary made clear. The *Wall Street Journal* came out in favor, but so was *Pravda,* no doubt because a return to gold would have proven a boon for the Soviet Union, a major gold exporter that would have benefitted enormously from the price increase that Rueff identified as the necessary accompaniment to any return to the gold standard. South Africa was another such case.

Like Rueff, De Gaulle was clearly concerned with France's inability to control inflation. Inflation had contributed to his failure to realize the post-war regime of his choice in 1945. In the 1950s and early 1960s, France had been forced to undergo repeated austerity plans, most of which involved price controls, in order to fight back one after another inflationary flareup. By 1964 the domestic possibilities for controlling inflation seemed to have failed. Rueff insisted the international monetary system was the real root of the problem.

In so far as the gold standard promised order and discipline, it thus also fit de Gaulle's conservative political values. However, de Gaulle also had motivations of his own that went beyond Rueff's anti-inflationary proselytizing. Economic nationalism was clearly one—a view Rueff would have had mixed feelings about. In the early 1960s, U.S. multinationals had been buying up French assets, bringing criticism from those who saw the activity as another arm of U.S. imperialism. General Motors had fired a number of French workers at one of its plants in 1962 and Chrysler had bought Simca in 1963. Both of these contributed to the view that the United States had undue influence in French economic affairs.

Indeed, on some level, the dollar's special role in the international monetary system touched on issues of national sovereignty. De Gaulle recognized the benefits of international commerce and as well as the fact that France would have to be competitive internationally if it were to sustain the economic base requisite for national power on the global scale. He refused to accept, however, that the management of domestic economic problems should be so influenced by the monetary policies of the United States. That the fate of a nation's economy should rest on decisions made in another country, no matter how important that country might be, was a direct affront to his deepest political convictions.

An international political economy that complemented de Gaulle's vision of international affairs would be based on national currencies. No state would be required to accept the monetary policies of other nations against its will, simply as a price of participation. De Gaulle no doubt also preferred the gold standard because it did not require supranational management. In short, the gold standard would enable international commerce to function, but discipline in the system would be maintained by the objective mechanism of gold rather than the International Monetary Fund or any other supranational body. At the same time, the United States would be forced to accept the same discipline as other states, and the resulting equality would be good not only for the prosperity of the system as a whole, but also for America. The latter was a point that Rueff returned to frequently in his many columns and speeches in these years.

DE GAULLE AND MONETARY CONSERVATISM TODAY

What is the relevance of this perspective for the international monetary and economic affairs today? As noted, de Gaulle's argument for a return to gold never had its intended impact. The world ended up with floating rates and a *de facto* dollar standard—precisely the opposite of what he sought. Of course, the first moves toward European Monetary Union were taken in the late 1960s as Bretton Woods was collapsing, but there is little evidence of a direct link between de Gaulle's arguments for a return to gold and these.

Nevertheless, the problem of the emerging dollar standard, to which de Gaulle and Rueff both drew attention in the 1960s, remains significant today. For one, deficits continue to create problems in international affairs, although now the concern over the U.S. deficit with Europe has given way to concern with the U.S. deficit with China. Should that deficit become the root of a trade war, the wisdom of de Gaulle and Rueff's conservative views will again seem clear.

At the same time, the United States continues to enjoy the ability to "export" dollars to cover these deficits. One side effect of this is a massive accumulation of dollars in foreign accounts—an accumulation so large as to be near unimaginable in the 1960s. This clearly poses a danger for the international financial system—what might be called dollar overhang *redux.* Holders of dollar assets are loathe to see the dollar collapse on account of the impact that it could have on their own balance sheets. This helps prop the dollar up. However, if the day should come when the U.S. creditors judge America's fiscal situation unsustainable and decide to write off their losses and turn tail, the impact on the system could be enormous. True, the adjustment could also be gradual as more and more countries choose to hold euro or other assets, but the risk is there nonetheless. Indeed, today's is precisely the situation Rueff and de Gaulle sought to avoid, though on terms more severe than those Rueff and de Gaulle imagined.

When it comes to inflation, the inherent wisdom of de Gaulle's conservatism is also worth note. In a crisis like the one that hit the world in late 2008, panic sets in and democratic countries normally grab at the faucet of deficit spending and monetary creation. Concern over the long-term consequences of policies that are inherently inflationary is cast aside in the fear of losing everything. It may well be that in a crisis, inflation is the best of a number of bad options, as Keynes's famous dictum on long- and short-term trade-offs suggests. But the wisdom of a present policy does not allow one to escape its damaging future consequences. Those countries that have chosen a comparatively restrained fiscal policy in the current crisis—Germany, for example—may well prove better off in the long run.

In the final analysis, even though de Gaulle's plan for a return to the gold standard had its technical and geopolitical drawbacks, it nevertheless pointed to a vision of international affairs in which states were equal at least in the sense that their economic fortunes were determined primarily by their own willingness to work and sacrifice for the future rather than consume for the present. It should be noted that this view, cut across the grain of postwar political economic policy in western Europe, which had embraced Fordism, rapid expansion, and American consumer culture as a means of placating the masses and ensuring against a return to the mob passions of the interwar period. Even if somewhat ideal, de Gaulle's remains an attractive one today. If nothing else, de Gaulle's vision continues to remind us of the extent to which power and basic issues of political order permeate even the most technical of arguments about international monetary arrangements. Would that more students of economics today were versed in his perspective.

SELECT BIBLIOGRAPHY

Calleo, David P. *The Imperious Economy.* Cambridge, MA: Harvard University Press 1982.
Chivvis, Christopher S. *The Monetary Conservative.* De Kalb: Northern Illinois University Press 2010.

Couve de Murville, Maurice. *Une Politique Etrangere.* Paris: Editions Plon 1971.

de Gaulle, Charles. *Memoirs d'Espoir.* Paris: Plon, 1970.

Giauque, Jeffery Glenn. *Grand Designs and Visions of Unity.* Chapel Hill: University of North Carolina Press, 2002.

Hayek, Friedrich. *The Road to Serfdom.* Chicago: University of Chicago Press, 1944.

James, Harold. *International Monetary Cooperation since Bretton Woods.* Oxford: Oxford University Press, 1996.

Kuisel, Richard. *Seducing the French.* Berkeley: University of California Press, 1997.

Lacouture, Jean. *De Gaulle,* vol. III, *Le Souverain.* Paris: Editions du Seuil, 1986.

Rueff, Jacques. *L'Ordre Social.* Paris: Plon, 1945.

———. *La Peche Monétaire de L'Occident.* Paris: Plon, 1971.

Chapter 3

Gaullist Economic Policies

The Role of Indicative Planning

Benjamin M. Rowland

INTRODUCTION

While history and culture have shaped economic ideas and practices in France into a different form from their perennial *anglo-saxon* rivals, France's economic performance does not seem to have suffered as a result. Actual economic results in postwar France have been as good or better than its European counterparts, in large measure because of the practice of progressively opening the national marketplace and inviting competition, But this broadly liberal economic framework contains more than a few echoes of France's *etatist* past, along with an inclusionist or, to use Stanley Hoffman's term, "neo-corporatist" approach to different national sectors and economic interests.

A few statistics confirm France's successful postwar record. Measured by exports and imports as a percentage of GDP, France is more than twice as open as the United States[1]. France is also second only to the UK as a site for foreign investment in Europe. One employed Frenchman in seven works for a foreign company. Forty percent of the shares in France's largest companies (those listed on the CAC 40) are held by foreign institutions and individuals. Yet France has achieved these results without forfeiting much of its distinct economic culture.

New Yorker essayist Adam Gopnik suggests that the French economic ideal, drawing on the nation's artisanal past, is one in which everyone is first and foremost a producer, "where everyone has a *métier* but no customers to trouble him." In the United States, the ideal would arguably be just the reverse, that is, a nation of consumers largely unconcerned with where goods were produced or the welfare of those who produced them.[2] Nonetheless, as the French economy has grown more integrated, first with Europe and then with the rest of the world, the French ideal of "producer sovereignty" has become harder and harder to defend.

This essay tells the story of indicative planning (*planning indicatif*), one of the most well-known economic experiments in postwar France—in effect, an effort by France to find a middle ground between *dirigisme* and the acknowledged benefits of an open liberal economy.

Indicative planning is a form of economic collaboration between the French public and private sectors based on information-sharing and supported by specific institutions and, especially in its early days, directed economic incentives. Its high point is generally agreed to be the ten-year period of de Gaulle's presidency (1958–1969). But its usefulness soon passed. By 1978, planning had given up any pretense of setting detailed numerical targets. Finally, in 2006, the *Comissarriat de Plan* ceased to have a separate identity and was absorbed into the *Centre de Analise Strategique,* an entity, attached to the Prime Minister's office similar to the U.S. Government's Council of Economic Advisors.

This chapter has two main objectives. First, how did indicative planning fit into the broader picture of French postwar economic and social policies? What forms and processes did it adopt? What can be said about planning's economic record? How was it regarded by de Gaulle himself?

The second purpose is to explore whether indicative planning offers anything useful to policymakers today. For many observers the economic crisis starting in 2007–2008 has put into play the liberal/rational market-expectations theories that have guided U.S. and many European economic policies for the last thirty or more years. In the United States, the public no less than the private sector is uncomfortable with the current state of affairs, sensing that any new boundary between the public and private economic domains remains to be drawn. Indicative planning suggests a different model, one where consultation, or to use the French term, *concertation,* between the public and private sectors can complement autonomous market forces. Whether indicative planning actually affected economic outcomes in France is debatable. Even if it did, the question of its transferability across borders would also need to be addressed. Is it a set of techniques that can be applied without regard to context? Or is French planning as some argue, "more French than planning," that is, more a product of French history and culture than of the application of general, objective principles?

THE PLANNING PROCESS

State involvement in the productive economy in France has a 350-year history, commencing with the Finance Minister to Louis XIV, Jean-Baptiste Colbert. Under Colbert and his successors, the State effectively micromanaged the country's merchants and small businessmen (dirigisme) through the application of detailed rules and regulations, mostly drawn up at the Center. The hand of the State was heavy, and there is little evidence of public-private sector dialogue.[3] Indicative planning, to the contrary, was premised on a continuous give and take between the Government and the private sector. The system evolved gradually during the thirty years of high economic performance, the *trente glorieuses,* following the end of World War II.[4]

Three main stages of indicative planning can be identified. First, in the years immediately following the war, the Government, backed by a near monopoly of credit including Marshall Plan aid, mainly determined what it wanted to do, and then informed the private sector of its decisions. The result was not pure Colbertian *dirigisme* since the private sector was not obliged to follow the Government's lead. Nonetheless, with the Government's preponderance of credit and readiness to use other economic incentives and disincentives, and the lack of a tradition of private-sector independence, it was a rare businessman who didn't go along with what the Government suggested.

During the second stage, coinciding with the last years of the Fourth Republic and the first years of the Fifth, an elaborate public-private consultative mechanism was gradually put in place, Given the public-private composition of the numerous commissions and subcommittees involved, private sector views most likely did have some impact on planning decisions. In a final stage, starting in the mid-sixties, the consulting mechanism of the plan grew to encompass more and more sectors and regions, but as its reach widened, its influence grew more shallow. The Plan's decline, ironically, was probably first and foremost a consequence of its greater breadth, the well-known phenomenon of failing to see the forest for the multiplicity of trees. But also involved were economic surprises such as the oil crises and the French economy's own growing openness to regional and global economic forces.

The origins of indicative planning lay in an act of bureaucratic organization brought on by a need to facilitate relations with the Americans. With liberation, the French government established an office within the Ministry of National Economy to coordinate overseas assistance. In January, 1946, on the recommendation of the French Mission in the United States that a stronger counterpart was needed, the Government combined several scattered offices and agencies into a single "Commissariat de Plan." And when Marshall Plan aid started to flow in 1947, accounting for as much as a third of all capital spending, it was distributed through the Commissariat, ensuring a central place for the office in the bureaucratic process.

Writing around the time of the Fourth Plan (1962–1965), the economic historian, Charles Kindleberger summarized how the Commissariat's work was organized and delivered.[5] A given Plan began with a prior government-wide agreement (chiefly the Commissariat and the Treasury) on an overall macroeconomic rate of growth. The Planning Commissariat itself was initially divided into three horizontal divisions, Economics, Finance and Regional, plus ten vertical sections: Agriculture, Energy, Water, Transport, Industry, Fisheries and Artisans, Construction, Housing, Urban Development, and Overseas Territories. Thus, for example there would be a different planning "box" or sub-plan for each of the economic, financial and regional concerns relating to agriculture, and so forth.

Specialized commissions were responsible for developing specific sub-plans and their number grew along with Plan's expanding scope. For example, the horizontal commissions were three for the Third Plan. By the time of the Fourth Plan these grew to five, including General Economics and Finance, Manpower, Productivity, Research, and Regional Plans. The vertical commissions, covering sectors, expanded from seven in the First Plan, to seventeen in the Third Plan, twenty-two in the Fourth and thirty-two in the Fifth.

The planning process typically began three years or more before a Plan's formal starting date. After consultations between the *Commisariat* and the Investment and Planning Section of the Economic and Social Council, an overall growth rate was adopted Then the government added its directives covering major goals, such as balance-of-payments or regional equilibrium, or education, housing, and urban redevelopment, These constituted the *Commisariat's* marching orders. Then, the commissions within the *Commisariat* would go to work to prepare detailed and consistent targets by sectors and industries. Used in the process were projections, detailed industry studies and other data including input-output tables, prepared elsewhere in the government. Year-end sector and industry targets were then broken down and built up again by an iterative process, shuttling back and forth between the horizontal and vertical commissions and working parties of the *commissariat* and the *commissariat* staff itself. All this took not only time but numerous experts. For example, Kindleberger estimated that some 3,000 people served with commissions and working parties on the Fourth Plan.

Each of the Plans, typically three or four years in duration, also had an overall defining focus. The First Plan, also called the Monnet Plan, (1947–1952) was more *dirigiste* than indicative, reflecting the concentration of resources, including Marshall Plan funds, in the Government's hands.[6] The Plan adopted the slogan "Modernization or Decadence" and centered on six basic sectors: coal, electricity, steel, cement, agricultural machinery, and transportation.

The Second Plan coincided with the waning years of the Fourth Republic (1954–1957). It added new sectors, including public investment in schools and hospitals, and had detailed production and investment targets, along with some reduction of restrictive practices to enable more foreign competition.

The Third Plan (1958–1961) commenced at the onset of the Fifth Republic and continued to add new tasks and sectors to the old ones. Inspired by the apparent success of its predecessors it was "more ambitious, elaborate, scientific and technical" than any of the preceding plans.[7] It overlapped, among other things, with the winding down of the Algerian Crisis and the launch of the Common Market. Its macroeconomic goal of total growth of 20 percent over the course of the planning period was easily met but at the expense of a badly deteriorating macro-economic environment. Whether planning was cause or effect of France's weak macro-economy fueled a seemingly endless debate among economists. In any event, having inherited a situation with rampant inflation and near zero reserves, de Gaulle, on entering office, devalued the currency by 19 percent and introduced a wage and price freeze, the so-called Pinay-Rueff Stabilization Plan.[8]

The Fourth Plan (1962–1965) set a growth target of 5.5 percent per annum, a full percentage point higher than what had been achieved in the previous planning period. Unlike earlier plans, the Fourth Plan also included specific social and redistributive goals. "The main purpose of the Plan was no longer the allocation of scarce resources (but) . . . more concerned with the problems of sharing out the fruits of expansion."[9]

In hindsight, by midway into the Fifth Plan (1965–1970), the high-water mark of French Planning had already come and gone. Although actual growth in this period exceeded Plan targets, the Plan itself took on an almost baroque character as it "aspired to interweave the needs and products of all French industrial sectors, in a grandiose, excessively complex input-output model."[10] By the Eighth Plan (1980–1984) the game was largely over. The Plan no longer contained quantitative targets because, as explained in the Plan's own introduction "this technique has been rendered obsolete by the fluctuations of a new era and the growing uncertainties that result from them."[11]

Plan:	Years	Forecast	Actual
Second:	1953–57	4.4	5.2
Third:	1957–61	4.9	4.5
Fourth:	1961–65	5.5	6.3
Fifth:	1965–70	5.0	5.8
Sixth:	1970–75	5.9	3.8
Seventh:	1975–80	5.2	3.8
Eighth:	1980–84	3.2–2.7	1.2
Ninth:	1984–88	2.2–1.6	1.1

(*Source: Wikipedia*, French Economic Planning)

DID PLANNING MAKE A DIFFERENCE?

Those looking to show quantitatively that Planning was effective quickly encountered a problem: there was no parallel France where Planning never took place; hence no base case or "counter-factual" against which the possible fruits of planning could be measured. Nonetheless, as noted above, this did not stop an extensive debate from taking place. In the overall debate, which Kindleberger characterized as "neuralgic," defenders of planning focused first and foremost on failures in the pricing system: "Sometimes it was thought that the price system produced the wrong amount, whether too much or too little capacity as separate firms, making their own forecasts of global demand, followed independent investment programs." Initially, Kindleberger continues, capital was thought to be scarce. Thus, indulging in the creative destruction of competitive capitalism would have given rise to excess capacity that the country could ill afford. Later, a majority of French economists feared that the problem was not over- but under-investment, while both views reflected France's basic distrust of anarchic competition. . . . Finally, French officials returned to the earlier view that private pricing leads to excessive investment and waste through unemployment as the factor of capital was excessively substituted for the factor of labor. Kindleberger concludes: "It is, of course, possible to reconcile these views with the position that the price system produces too little investment in noncompetitive industries . . . and too much in competitive. In these circumstances planning calls simultaneously for more competition and less, with each therapy applied separately. It is hard to find an explicit statement of this point of view, but it may well be implicit in the contradictions that abound in writing on this subject."[12]

France suffered from macro-economic imbalances until the 1959 Pinay-Rueff Stabilization Plan, cited above, but instability started up again only a few years later. Against this unimpressive macro-economic record, one way to justify planning was as a way for the State to meet certain of its objectives, such as export expansion, despite an overvalued currency and an economy in basic disequilibrium. But the opposite point of view is also possible, that is, that planning, with its focus on accelerated growth, created more problems for macro-economic policy than vice-versa.

DE GAULLE AND PLANNING

De Gaulle's ideas on planning and on economics in general, were grounded in the notion that the interests of the State—a sort of General Will visible clearly only to himself—were paramount. As long as State primacy was honored, de Gaulle's specific economic ideas could be highly variable, favoring whatever set of practices had the potential in a dynamic world to maximize State power. Speaking on the nationalization of several basic sectors of the French economy at the end of the War—coal, electricity finance, and so on—de Gaulle comments, "I had conceived a Plan that was nothing more than common sense,"[13] it being in his judgment clear beyond argument that only the State could mobilize the necessary resources for reconstruction and recovery. The private sector, spoiled and timid from years of protection during the interwar years was in no condition to lead this task: "The French," de Gaulle wrote, "suffer from a deep-seated sickness. They will not understand that the times demand of them a gigantic task. They cannot do without the State and yet they detest it, except when there is a danger. They do not behave like adults."[14] They had to be re-oriented by finding a kind of third way between Communism and Capitalism.[15]

De Gaulle's distrust of the private sector and free markets was a constant that ran throughout his years in office. In an April 1963 press conference on economic policy, a year when the economy was doing well and planning's reputation arguably at its height, de Gaulle's language was unrepentantly dirigiste: "The duty of the public authorities is to see that the rules and the limits (of the Plan) are respected, without which everything will be compromised. Naturally each individual and each profession wants to obtain more. . . . This implies that the Government itself be organized, in its technical councils and its administration, in order to study, appraise and decide with a fuller knowledge of what is happening. But above all and beyond anything, this implies that the State should hold the reins, that it should be the force that raises the waves but also the dike that holds back the tides and that—far from allowing the streams of demagogy to appear on all sides, to swell, to become uncontrollable torrents, until the house is engulfed by the flood—it should continue to lead the country in accordance with the rules of the Plan."[16]

SHOULD THE UNITED STATES PRACTICE INDICATIVE PLANNING?

The clearest parallel between France under the Plan and the United States in the grip of the current economic crisis is that both governments, for a period of time, have had an effective monopoly on the allocation of credit., France during the period of the Marshall Plan and the United States at least briefly following the collapse of Lehman Brothers in the fall of 2008. In comparison to France, however, the U.S. Executive has either been unwilling, partisan characterizations notwithstanding, to seize the power that is potentially a part of such a position. This may be in part a consequence of some of the main differences between the French and U.S. political systems. With its relatively weak Executive, dependent, in the case of important issues on congressional super majorities, the United States simply lacks the means to "concert" the vast number of interest groups that find fertile soil in the K Street lobbies and their friends in Congress and elsewhere. A Presidential referendum, if it existed, could override partisan gridlock, but of course no such mechanism exists at the national level in the American political system. Moreover, the tool itself may be too blunt, opening the door to the "mob rule" much feared by the founding fathers when they contemplated a political system in the hands of a pure democracy. Reflecting on these differences between France and the United States, one can find in remarks by former Federal Reserve Chairman Alan Greenspan a perhaps representative statement of how the role of government in the economy is viewed in the United States:

> Any significant role for the Government in capital allocation risks undermining the process of "creative destruction"—the private sector market competition that is essential to rising standards of living. This paradigm's reputation has been badly tarnished by recent events. Improvements in financial regulation and supervision, especially in areas of capital adequacy, are necessary. However, for the best chance for worldwide economic growth we must continue to rely on private market forces to allocate capital and other resources. The alternative of political allocation of resources has been tried; and it failed.[17]

A Frenchman reading Greenspan's remarks might well feel that he is too caught up in a bipolar economic world, much as the U.S. government has been in the area of grand strategy. Indicative planning, at its best, suggested a willingness to experiment with the lines of demarcation between the public and private sectors as circumstances might require. A more mature U.S. society might still grow into adopting at least some of the features (dialogue, for one) of this reasonable posture. For the time being, it seems too much to ask.

NOTES

1. Some 70 percent of France's trade and investment occur within the European Community. If one discounts the EC amounts, United States, and French openness are much more alike.

2. Adam Gopnik, *Paris to the Moon* (New York: Random House, 2000). "When the waiter at the café finally deigns to shake your hand, it does not mean that you are now a valued client. It means that you are now an honorary waiter," op. cit., p. 125.

3. During Colbert's tenure, the French government is said to have killed some 16,000 small entrepreneurs for violating the laws for the production of cotton cloth. Hernando de Soto, *The Mystery of Capitalism* (New York: Basic Books, 2000). Cited in *Wikipedia*, Jean-Baptiste Colbert.

4. Jean Fouristie, *Les Trente Glorieuses ou la Revolution Invisible de 1946 a 1970* (Paris: Fayard, 1979).

5. Charles P. Kindleberger, "French Planning," not dated.

6. From 1947–1952, 51 percent of national investment in France came from public funds, including Marshall Plan aid. Mairi Maclean, Economic Management and French Business (London: Palgrave, 2002), 66.

7. Maclean, op. cit. p. 78.

8. Never a strong believer in planning, Rueff likened the technique to "the cockrel who believes his crowing causes the sun to rise." Maclean, op. cit. p. 80.

9. Maclean, op. cit. p. 79.

10. Maclean, op. cit. p. 80.

11. Maclean, op. cit., p. 247 note 6.

12. Kindleberger, op. cit.

13. Charles de Gaulle, *Salvation, 1944–1946*, (London: Weidenfeld and Nicolson, 1960), pp. 232–33.

14. De Gaulle frequently invoked the image of the French populace as spoiled children, such as the following in the context of the Algerian uprising: "Some fools have complained about 'my inconsistencies.' As though the World in which I had to act hadn't changed! As if a consistent policy was always the same. They must suppose that living consists in imitating childhood, wanting jam at any price!" Malraux, *Felled Oaks: Conversations with de Gaulle* (New York: Holt, Rinehart and Winston, 1971), p. 111.

15. "I don't see why an economic system called Communism shouldn't be better than another called Capitalism. I don't like 'isms.'" Malraux, op. cit. p. 91.

16. De Gaulle, press conference, April 19, 1963. In 1961, Pierre Massé, *Commissaire General du Plan*, on reading the draft of a speech on planning being prepared by de Gaulle, came upon the words, "the State must direct the economy." Massé proposed replacing "direct" (*diriger*) with "orient" (*orienter*), to which de Gaulle allegedly retorted, "it's direct or nothing," then, on reflection, consented to use the verb "conduct" (*conduire*). *Maclean*. op. cit. p. 240.

17. *Financial Times*, June 26, 2009.

Chapter 4

The General and Germany

Michael Stuermer

General de Gaulle had always had, as he famously wrote, a certain idea of France. But from his early days as a young infantry officer somewhere in the provinces until the waning days of his presidency half a century later, his concept of France's destiny also implied a certain, though changing, idea of Germany. The tragedy of France and the tragedy of Germany were to shape the mind and soul of Charles de Gaulle much as, when the time came, his policies. When president, he travelled to Russia and visited the city of Stalingrad. "*Un grand peuple,*" he exclaimed. When the Russians wanted to hear more, he added: "*Qu'ils sont venus jusqu'ici.*"

One can imagine de Gaulle, once he had assumed the leadership of France, reflecting upon the strange debt he owed to Germany. There was a grim irony in his rise to be the savior of France. For without the defeat of France in 1940 at the hands of the Wehrmacht, he would not have had a chance to step forward, speak over the BBC—"France has lost a battle, but not the war"—assume the mantle of national leader, and become the savior of the nation. Instead, de Gaulle would have remained forever a disgruntled, difficult military man whose books, full of caveats and vision, might have gone unread, finally spending a quiet and boring pensioner's life in Colombey les Deux Eglises. Instead, fate took an unexpected turn, and he rose to become a world leader, the conqueror of Paris first from the Germans and the Communists and then from the Fourth Republic and, in the last and final act, the incarnation of the French nation.

Having been born into a devoutly Catholic and conservative family of lower nobility—how could a young man of this time and place escape from the predicament of European civilization when nation states and far flung empires vied for power and control of vast parts of the globe?

33

Young Charles de Gaulle saw his calling in the army, having been taught, in early childhood at school, to sing an outspoken song: *"Enfant tu seras soldat. . . ."*

It was the time when France tried to copy many of the institutions, from the school system to the church and the army, that had enabled the Prussians to conquer not only the Austrians, Hanover, and most of the South Germans in 1866, but also France only a few years later, challenging the very country that had seen itself as the natural master of the European continent, a light to the nations, rich and strong both in war and peace. The depth of French humiliation and of every French patriot can only be measured against the high tide of arrogance and anxiety that had inspired the era of Napoleon III and imbued it with playful exuberance in the arts, capitalist growth in the economy much as with military expansion across the oceans, playing the arbiter of the continent and taking the rest of Europe for granted.

The French Third Republic, heir to the 1789 and the 1848 revolutions, and the German Reich that was Prussia writ large across the center of Europe were born together in the grey, traumatic winter days of *"l'année maudite,"* as the painter Honoré Daumier put it succinctly. Almost simultaneously Bismarck had his King pronounced German Emperor in the Sun King's Hall of Mirrors while the *Gouvernement de Bordeaux* fought a merciless battle against the insurgents of Paris, ending with mass executions at the *"mur des Federés"* on the margins of the historic graveyard Père Lachaise and countless sentences to lifelong imprisonment on Devil's Island. The de Gaulle family may have taken those disasters with a stiff upper lip. But their son was to volunteer for military service, expecting that one day, when France was no longer alone, there would surely be a day of *revanche.*

France's Second Empire had died a sudden death on the battlefields near Sedan, Napoleon III was discredited and gone, the Paris Commune slaughtered, the bourgeois republic both triumphant at home and humiliated on the European stage. Meanwhile the Iron Chancellor hammered the new Germany together around the hard core of Prussia, using a methodology of both "blood and iron" and "gold and iron." In all of this, Bismarck combined brute force, industrial prowess, wartime passions, and, for good measure, delicate corruption, when he administered a hefty sum of silver thalers to the Bavarian king to make him sign the letter—he even obliged the king by providing the draft—that was to invite, and legitimize, the Prussian cousin to graciously accept the Imperial title.

However, the catastrophic beginnings of the Third Republic were overcome much faster than anybody could have expected. The Republic, deeply divided along the lines of Orleanists, Bonapartists and the left never managed to adopt a proper constitution, resigning itself to some organic laws that divided effective government between a weak figurehead president and a strong parliament. To keep everything together, Frenchmen could rely on a strong and proud administration—the *grands corps*—and army. In the absence of national consensus at home, it was the idea of *revanche* that united the nation, that would redraw the map of Europe once France had overcome its diplomatic isolation and military weakness. The reparations imposed in 1871 by the victors in the Frankfurt Peace Treaty were quickly paid up—in fact the French state credit, in spite of the war, was so strong that the loans were oversubscribed thirteen times, not least in Germany. Soon the Prussian occupation troops withdrew to the new borders, with Metz and Strasbourg now being on the German side, and the river Meuse serving as France's moat against another Prussian onslaught, with Sedan and Verdun soon to be massively fortified. The annexation of Alsace and Lorraine—for the French the lost daughters on the Rhine, represented on the Place de la Concorde with a permanent black veil—was, unwittingly, a moral gift to the French who otherwise might not have found much common ground. France was deeply divided in social and political terms, and those cleavages had been laid bare through the three wars of 1870/1871—the war of the Empire, the war of the Loire, and the war of the Commune. The bitterness over the annexation did indeed help the French to reorganize themselves as a nation. Nobody, from the monarchist far right to the communist radical left, would or could possibly consider reconciling France with the amputation of the two provinces. To accept the loss as a permanent feature would have been tantamount to political suicide. On the contrary, by keeping the patriotic fervor alive, Frenchmen could unite against the enemy *outre Rhin.*

But something unexpected happened. While for the French navy, remembering Abukir and Trafalgar, the British were the measure of supremacy, the French army was fixated on the Prussian military, the use of technology, especially the railways, the introduction of state-of-the-art weaponry, and the copying of massive artillery fire. No amount of colonial expansion could ever make the French of the *Belle Epoque* forget *"la ligne bleue des Vosges."* At the turn of the century, it was this ambiguity between lingering war and the enthusiasm of progress and civilization that seems to have formed the mindset of the young lieutenant about to embark on a military career.

During the previous two decades, the balance of forces had begun to move. In the summer of 1875, when Berlin journals raised the question of another, pre-emptive war against French rearmament, the European powers, notably London and St. Petersburg, made clear their utter displeasure. It did not enhance Bismarck's standing that he was suspected to have provided the inspiration.

But more was to come. In 1876/1877 the Russians intervened in the Balkans and crushed Turkish resistance to their military steamroller. In the peace treaty of San Stefano, they dictated to the diplomats of the High Porte brutal demands, carving out a large piece of land bypassing the Bosporus and calling it Bulgaria. Britain's Prime Minister Benjamin Disraeli, The Earl of Beaconsfield, threatened war, sent the Marines to Malta and some battleships of the Royal Navy into the Black Sea and secured from the Sultan the island of Cyprus as a naval base.

War was imminent between Russia and Great Britain, and the Great Powers of the day would have been drawn into the affair inexorably. This is why Bismarck, after much hesitation, decided to convoke a diplomatic conference to settle those dangerous Balkan questions. He pretended to be "the honest broker who wants to clinch a deal." And he did. But the Russians felt let down. Bismarck had not honored the spirit of Russia's blank check issued in 1870 when the Czar's government allowed Prussia to defeat the armies of Imperial France. Bismarck believed he could rely on the solidarity of the thrones, and postrevolutionary France and czarist Russia would never nestle with each other. But it was in the wake of the Berlin Congress that Bismarck lost Russia. In addition, German agriculture pressed for protective customs that were bound to hit Russia hard and all but curtail her ability to service the Russian debt—the latter largely in German hands. Thereafter, the Franco-Russian alliance was in the making. George F. Kennan the diplomat-historian described the Berlin Congress and Russian alienation as the point of departure for "the great seminal catastrophe of our century."

The Franco Russian alliance, first informal and, since the 1890s, a full-blown military and commercial alliance, was underpinned by a cozy financial relationship that was to channel, right down to the revolution, much French capital into Russian railways and other assets. The alliance between the radical republic and the reactionary Eastern Empire went through ups and downs, not because of ideological differences but because of Russia's Eastern expansion, the "Great Game" with Britain, and the attempts by subsequent German governments to repair the damage. But, once Great Britain had concluded the Entente Cordiale in 1904—ostensibly over African rivalries, but substantially to contain the rising power of the German Reich—the outline of the Great War could be discerned. And still, the sequence of events from the assassination of the Hapsburg crown prince and his wife on June 28 in Sarajevo to all-out war among the major European powers on August 4, 1914, was not inevitable.

All of a sudden Charles de Gaulle found himself in a hero's role, but not for long. In the bloodmill of Verdun, he had the good fortune instead of being killed only to be lightly wounded and taken prisoner. He spent the rest of the war in the disused historic fortress of Ingolstadt on the Danube, found time to read and to write and reflect upon the vicissitudes of history and the dictates of geography.

Immediately after the war Captain de Gaulle went back to France, changed uniforms and volunteered to join the staff of General Weygand in what was now, carved out of former German and Russian provinces, the Polish Republic. French forces were supporting not only the Polish effort to conquer vast swathes of Lithuania and Ukraine, but were also out to support the White Russians as they offered at least the slimmest of chances that prewar debts would one day be repaid, whereas the Bolsheviks did not show the slightest inclination to conform to financial rectitude.

Those years between armistice in the West and the consolidation of the Soviet regime were a defining moment for the future balance of power, but also a time for study for the well-read young officer in the *etat majeur*. Inevitably, the Eastern battlefields held not only the decision over who would control the great North European plains but also over the future role of Germany. The Kaiser's armies were defeated, no doubt. But if the Bolsheviks won in the Russian civil war, and if the new Poland remained squeezed between a strong and resentful Russia and a strong and resentful Germany, France's European hegemony would be an empty gesture, in fact entirely dependent on the continuing military and diplomatic support of what de Gaulle later in life would call, with no small amount of *ressentiment*, "*les Anglo-Saxons*." The French expeditionary force under General Weygand was indeed fighting not for Poland or for Russia's Whites, but for a map of Europe under the lasting domination of France.

If this was, parallel to the Paris Peace Conference, the Eastern part of French Grand Strategy, it failed almost completely. The Polish armies, after having galloped as far as Kiew on the Dniepr, were driven back by the Red Army, and it needed the "miracle of the vistula"—ascribed, in Polish lore, to the black Madonna of Czenstochau, but in reality owed very largely to the military genius of General Pilsudski—to save Poland from the brutal revenge of the Russians. What remained was the "Petite Entente" formed by France around Weimar Germany and what remained of Austria. A few years on, the last U.S. soldiers would have left Europe, and Britain, instead of permanently protecting France and her nightmares from Germany, had great pains to reconstruct at least part of the Empire, control Mesopotamia and Palestine, keep India quiet, and oppose the Soviet Union's reconquest of much of Central Asia, Persia, and the approaches to India. France, "*sanglée blanc*" as the French described their physical and moral state after the Great War, was isolated, expecting the worst from Germany and no ready help from across the water. It was in this situation that the concept of fortified defenses on the Eastern border was developed by French military planners and approved by the *Assemblée Nationale* known as the *Ligne Maginot,* named after the defense minister responsible. Instead of the trenches of the Great War a wall of steel and concrete would save treasure and blood and deter a resurgent Germany from seeking a third round of battle.

Major de Gaulle strongly disagreed and predicted that, given the revolution in military affairs that was taking place static defense would be the road to disaster. By now he was almost an adopted son of Marechal Petain, of Verdun fame, for whom he wrote long memoranda on the war of the future. But it was to no avail. De Gaulle found himself the odd man out, preaching a theory of tank warfare in combination with air power that found no takers among French generals. He had studied the classic "On War" by Carl von Clausewitz and understood very well that, unlike trench warfare of the past, the new technologies offered a way to maneuver with speed in three dimensions and to form ever-changing points of gravity. That required, instead of scattered tanks across many infantry divisions, the concentration of tanks in fast-moving brigades, supported by air power and infantry. It was no accident that those theories ran parallel to what at the same time German military men were conceptualizing and indeed putting into practice, together with the Red Army, in Soviet Russia. One of those officers was Guderian whose books and articles de Gaulle, fluent in both German and English, would study. But time was running out. De Gaulle was too junior to effect a serious change of French strategy, and the German danger did not seem to be all that urgent. If France wanted to keep the *Departements d'Outre Mer* in North Africa as well as the colonies in Africa and Indochina, the military establishment would have to spread its forces very thinly across half the globe. De Gaulle, with his heroic pessimism, his thorough knowledge of German strengths and weaknesses, and his close-up experience on the Eastern European battlefields was a lonely voice in the wilderness of French strategic planning.

The years of the Great Depression and the *"Front Populaire"* in power were not auspicious for a military man who had a reputation of being difficult, immutable, and outspoken. All those qualities did not endear the Colonel de Gaulle to his superiors. However, when the time came, he was entrusted with commanding one of the very few tank units the French army had. The *"drole de guerre"* in 1939/1940 gave him time to put theory into practice. During the short and disastrous six weeks campaign of early summer, 1940, when France was defeated and ready to capitulate, de Gaulle was one of the few French military leaders to hold his own. In return, he was promoted to brigadier general—*"a titre temporaire"*—and called into the war ministry. While on one of the last diplomatic missions to London during the days of armistice he made himself the spokesman for France. On the BBC, on June 18, exactly 125 years after the battle of Waterloo or *"Belle Alliance"* in

German military tradition, he stated over the airwaves that France had lost a battle but that the war would go on until victory. Probably not very many people in France at the time heard the message, nor would they know who "*moi, le General de Gaulle*" really was. But whatever the perception at the time, the general had rebelled against the government's decision to conclude an armistice and sue for peace, and there could be no return for him or anybody around him. From now on it was a question not only of how to deal with the German invaders, but also of who would represent the authentic voice of France. De Gaulle, so far a maverick inside the "*armée de terre,*" was now, according to the government at Vichy, a traitor; to others, a leader of the—almost nonexistent—Free French Forces and a hope for a better future. De Gaulle saw himself, according to his entourage, as a new incarnation of Jeanne d'Arc. Whatever his self image and his standing with the resistance, he was, by no means, accepted by allied war leaders as their one and only counterpart on the French side. In fact he had to establish his own authority against much competition from France as well as against the doubts of first "*les Anglo-Saxons,*" meaning Churchill and Roosevelt, and later Stalin. Behind the fight for position, there was the much larger issue of whether one day France would sit among the vanquished, or the victors. There was also a highly personal element involved. *Marechal* Petain, the former mentor of de Gaulle and by now president of the *État Français,* run from Berlin and from Vichy, saw in de Gaulle a traitor. The General in London returned the compliment. Inside what began to be termed the Second World War there was something akin to a French civil war, defined by the question of being for or against Nazi Germany.

De Gaulle never forgave the Western allies that they had failed to invite him to their war conferences. But he took his own revenge. In 1944, when the allied armies finally fought their way out of the Normandy beaches and on to the Ruhr area, Germany's industrial heartland, the allied Supremo Dwight D. Eisenhower had little patience with de Gaulle's constant demand that the liberation of Paris was paramount—because he feared a communist takeover or a *tabula rasa* by the Wehrmacht, or both. For him, being first in Paris would secure not only legitimacy but also real control. In fact, it was Chaban-Delmas who negotiated an honorable peace with the German commander, General von Choltitz, both sides united in the wish to preserve the city of Paris and to keep the communists at bay—if necessary through silent collusion.

Having secured the script and the execution of "*liberation,*" de Gaulle proceeded to having another revenge. He went to Moscow and negotiated with Stalin what he termed "*la belle et bonne alliance.*" Of course he knew about the deep misgivings Churchill entertained about the unsavory ally in the East, while he also doubted American willingness to put up a counter-weight to Soviet predominance over the future of Europe. But the enthusiasm over France's new ally did not last long. At Yalta, in February 1945, Stalin indicated that France should not be admitted among the victors but be seen on the same level as Poland. It was only through Churchill, who never joined in the frenzied American "Uncle Joe"–delusion, that a major role was reserved for France. But throughout the rest of his life de Gaulle never tired of demanding "*sortir de Yalta.*" It was only after the "unconditional surrender" of the Wehrmacht that France, still without its own zone of occupation, was given an official and equal part in the Four Power declaration of June 5, 1945, on taking over "supreme power in Germany." At the Potsdam conference however, only six weeks later, no seat was reserved for the French chief of government and head of state. De Gaulle was furious—and would never forgive. Both his later nuclear policies, including the distances he marked towards NATO, as well as his insistence that in the last resort it is only the nation states that matter, have their origins in the object lessons drawn from what he termed—following Raymond Aron in 1944—"*la guerre de trente ans de notre siècle,*" and, more specifically, from being let down by allies he himself had never fully trusted—and would never trust.

It did not take long for de Gaulle to find his self respect incompatible with the political "*café de commerce*" of the political parties in postwar Paris. After less than two years he withdrew to Colombey les deux Eglises, a brooding presence thereafter, directing his party from afar and waiting for the downfall of the Fourth Republic. He let it be known: "*L'homme des grandes temp ê tes n'est pas celui pour les petites combinaisons.*"

There were indeed tempestuous times when he returned from his self-imposed exile in Lorraine to the Elysée and the commanding heights. "*Il faut faire le travail d'un psychiatre.*" Cutting zeroes from the currency and giving Paris a good wash changed appearances. However, cancelling the nuclear collaboration with Germany agreed between France's Defense Minister Chaban Delmas and Germany's Franz Josef Strauss was indicative of a new and autonomous Grand Strategy. "*Le nucleaire se partage mal*"—de Gaulle said in the direction not only of the Germans but also of the Americans, preparing the exit of French forces from NATO's integrated command—which did indeed take place in 1966, resulting in long-lasting strategic alienation between France and NATO. Technically, while NATO went for the Harmel Report and its dual strategy of "Deterrence and Détente," complemented by a counterforce strategy in the nuclear sphere, France was left with the choice of subordinating its nuclear forces to NATO and the United States—or of choosing its own strategic role. The General opted for the latter. Thereafter, French nuclear forces enhanced France's negotiating power vis-à-vis not only the Russians but also the Americans. Germany was relegated, once again, to second rank.

Georges Pompidou, de Gaulle's lieutenant, once remarked that Germany had the Deutschmark "*et nous avons notre bombinette.*"

Meanwhile, the European Economic Community (EEC) was seen more or less as a force multiplier for France in economic terms and a wide market for French agriculture, much as German industry welcomed the EEC as a wider market. While the Germans perceived the EEC as a way to overcome as much as possible the nation state, French philosophy was to preserve as much as possible of the nation state. "Ever closer union" was the compromise formula put into the preamble of the Treaty of Rome—and nobody ever dared to spell out exactly what this meant, neither General nor Chancellor.

There were many unspoken assumptions about the different national aspirations and security concerns. They came to the fore when Adenauer and de Gaulle concluded the Elysée Treaty in 1963: de Gaulle wanted to harness German industrial power to the overambitious project of a French Europe, while Adenauer wanted to bind the Germans into his "*Westorientierung*" and prevent the French from ever playing the Russian card against Germany. In the end, the Bundestag added a preamble expressing the absolute priority of the transatlantic link for Germany. De Gaulle never forgave and responded with his famous remark about treaties: they are like the roses and the smile of the young girls, they last as long as they last.

The two old men were both in their different ways, fathers of their fatherlands. They greatly respected each other, while never becoming too close, let alone allowing each other first names and *tutoiement.* They knew how to invoke the bitterness of the past in order to glorify the achievements of the present. They also knew that they had a bargain that was mutually advantageous: France had a German glacis and maintained, in Berlin and in everything concerning "Germany as a whole" along the Potsdam formula the victor's posture. Until 1990 a French ambassador could say, while in Berlin: "*Nous sommes souvereign ici.*" In return, Franco-German reconciliation helped not only the German economy but also proved to the world that the Germans by now happened to be with the good guys. There was also, just in case the Anglo Saxons should ever leave the European continent, Adenauer's statement, unofficial though it was, that the Atlantic and even the Channel gave Britain and the United States some maneuvering space, while geography would forever bind France and Germany together.

In the long run, however, Adenauer and de Gaulle were unable to change the strategic realities on the ground, Germany divided, with the Western sectors of Berlin in a precarious and potentially deadly situation, the Red Army with forty crack divisions entrenched in the Eastern part of the divided country, and France hiding behind the NATO *dispositif* across West Germany, deploying nuclear-tipped missiles with a reach not much beyond the Iron Curtain and certain to turn, if ever fired, the Eastern part of Germany into a wasteland. Both sides avoided public discussion carefully, as it would have exposed the raw structure of French security-thinking and the limits of the much celebrated *couple Franco-Allemand.* Both sides were—and remained—caught in the realities of European geography and extended nuclear deterrence.

BIBLIOGRAPHY

Aron, Raymond. *Histoire et Politique: Textes et temoignages.* Paris: Julliard, 1984.

Bloch, Charles. *Die Dritte Französische Republik.* Stuttgart: K. F. Koehlen, 1972.

Buchan, Alastair, and Philip Windsor. "Arms and Stability in Europe: A British-French-German Enquiry." *Studies in International Security* 6. London: Chatto & Windus for the Institute for Strategic Studies, 1963.

Cobban, Alfred. *A History of Modern France.* Harmondsworth, UK: Penguin Books, 1965.

Duval, Marcel, et Yves Le Baut. *L'arme nucleaire francaise.* Paris: Kronos, 1992.

Froment-Meurice, Henri. *Une puissance nommé Europe.* Paris: Juillard, 1984.

Grosser, Pierre. *The Western Alliance: European-American Relations since 1945.* London, Macmillan, 1980.

Lacouture, Jean. *De Gaulle,* 3 vols. Paris: Broché, 1984.

McNeil, William H. *The Pursuit of Power.* Chicago: University of Chicago Press, 1982.

Meacham, John. *Franklin and Winston: An Intimate Portrait of an Epic Friendship.* New York: Random House, 2003.

Nolte, Ernst. *Deutschand und der Kalte Krieg.* Stuttgart: Klett-Cotta, 1985.

Peyrefitte, Alain. *C'etait de Gaulle.* Paris: Gallimard, 1994.

Rhodes, Richard. *The Making of the Atom Bomb.* New York: Simon & Schuster, 1988.

Sauzay, Brigitte. *Le Vertige Allemand.* Essai. Paris: Olivier Orband, 1985.

Schunck, Peter. *Charles de Gaulle.* Berlin: Propyläen Verlag, 1998.

Schwarz, Hans-Peter. *Der pathetische Gigant: General de Gaulle de Gaulle.* In: H.-P. Schwarz, *Das Gesicht des Jahrhunderts,* pp. 203–18. Munich: Beck, 1998.

Weisenfeld, Ernst. *Charles de Gaulle: Der Magier im Elysée.* Munich: Beck, 1990.

Chapter 5

De Gaulle and the Italians

Thomas Row

Italy and the Italians do not loom especially large in the writings and speeches of Charles de Gaulle. Nor, when one turns to the secondary literature on de Gaulle is the treatment of Italy particularly developed.[1] The large biography by Jean Lacouture, for example, makes scant reference at all to the Italians.[2] The one useful publication dedicated to this topic is *"De Gaulle et l'Italie"* a collection of papers deriving from a conference on that subject organized by the École Française de Rome on the occasion of the centenary of de Gaulle's birth in 1990.[3]

In order to get a grasp of de Gaulle's thoughts about Italy and the Italians one needs, more often than not, to pry beneath the surface. A related question has to do with de Gaulle's actions towards the Italians—and these actions—or policies, of course, reflect and reveal his thoughts. The two periods where de Gaulle directly shaped French policy towards Italy were 1940–1946 and 1958–1969, and of these two it is the former, the period of the war, in which de Gaulle's thought and action concerning Italy is most pronounced and most consequential.

In my spoken remarks to the conference I attempted to map out the various dimensions of the broad question of "De Gaulle and the Italians." In this short written text, however, I will focus on the thought and action of de Gaulle towards the Italians during the Second World War. Rather than attempt a general narrative, I will focus on three key "moments" where de Gaulle's history and Italy's came together dramatically. These are June 10, 1940, when Italy declared war on France; September 8, 1943, when the Italian armistice was announced without France's participation; and the spring of 1945 when France occupied the Italian region of the Val d'Aosta. How did de Gaulle view the Italians? What were his policies towards them? How did these relate to his larger picture of international politics?

DE GAULLE AND THE ITALIANS AT WAR

When De Gaulle viewed Italy during the war, he did so from within a broad intellectual framework that he had developed over many years. It may be characterized by the following points[4]:

(a) Rome (Republic and Empire) and the Roman Catholic Church were the sources, along with the idea of personal liberty, of European civilization. Italy was a direct heir of the ancient Roman and Roman Catholic legacies.
(b) The modern Italian nation state, on the other hand, was something very new, inexperienced and underdeveloped. That young state, moreover, was in France's debt: not only for 1859 when France helped make unification possible, but for 1917–1918 when French troops went to the Piave to help save Italy after Caporetto.
(c) Fascism was a consequence of the immaturity of the Italian nation-state which was unable to cope with its disappointments after the First World War. Fascism was nothing but a dictatorship, and as such was doomed to fail. The alliance between Latin Italy and the Germans was something that went against the laws of nature. Being unnatural, it too would fail.

JUNE 10, 1940

June 10, 1940, was a day that would mark the destinies of both France and Italy. For Charles de Gaulle it was "a day of agony." The military, political, and moral collapse of France in the face of the German invasion had reached a point of no return. Militarily, the German armies had crossed the Seine below Paris, and the capital was doomed. Politically, the premier, Paul Reynaud, waffled, while the commander-in-chief, General Weygand, believing the situation to be hopeless, planned for an armistice. As de Gaulle recalled:

> The obvious fact of collapse was now borne in on all minds. But at the top of the state the tragedy was being played through as though in a dream. At certain moments one might even have thought that a sort of terrible humour was seasoning the fall of France, as she rolled from the crest of history down to the deepest hollow of the abyss.[5]

Late that night the government and de Gaulle left Paris; he would not return for four years.

On that same day Fascist Italy declared war on France and Britain. Addressing a "dispirited and unwarlike" crowd from the balcony of Palazzo Venezia, the Duce announced his great decision to enter the war and thus bound his and his country's fate to that of Nazi Germany.[6] When the war had broken out in 1939, Mussolini had kept Italy on the sidelines despite his formal ties to Germany. The country was neither militarily nor industrially prepared for war—and remained so. But with Germany's striking charge west in the spring of 1940, the situation had changed. Mussolini now feared that the war might soon be over without him and that Italy's ambitions would be denied. Those ambitions, aiming to assure Italian dominance in the Mediterranean, were to be achieved at the expense of Britain and France. Thus, as Charles de Gaulle was leaving Paris, the Italian nation was called to war against France. As President Roosevelt put it while speaking at the University of Virginia: "On this tenth day of June, 1940, the hand that held the dagger has struck it into the back of its neighbor."

In his memoirs, de Gaulle dwells little on the Italian declaration of war. Rather, he places it in the vein of "terrible humor (that) was seasoning the fall of France":

> So it was that, that morning, the Italian ambassador, M. Guariglia, came to the Rue Sant-Dominique on a somewhat strange visit. He was received by Badouin, who reported what the diplomat said as follows: "You will see that the declaration of war will in the end clarify relations between our two countries! It creates a situation from which, when all is said and done, much good will come"[7]

On June 10, Mussolini's decision must have seemed to the French like just another—and not entirely unexpected—piece of bad news. The weightier matters were the German invasion, the talks with the British, and the consideration of which decisions were to be taken by the wobbly French government itself. In the event, the Italian military were not ready for war. The attack finally came three days after the French asked for an armistice on June 18; in the Alpine campaign, thirteen small villages were captured.

Neither the ruthlessness of Mussolini's aims, nor the anger of de Gaulle's response should be underestimated. According to Denis Mack Smith, Mussolini aimed to reduce France to the rank of a second-class power, and thought that "Italy's welfare would depend upon France remaining permanently in a state of subjection."[8] The historian Odile Rudelle has studied de Gaulle's wartime speeches regarding Italy. After June 10, he gave free reign to his anger towards the Italians. The language is ferocious and delightful. Its main weapons are ridicule and derision, and the main theme is that if Hitler is a lion,

Mussolini is a jackal. This language, as Rudelle writes, had but one purpose: to make it perfectly clear that the Free French are not fooled by fascist ambitions and that no one in London should take Mussolini's Mediterranean pretensions seriously. France and its empire would not be touched.[9]

From the events of June 10, 1940, and from de Gaulle's account in his memoirs of that period (*The Fall*), we can draw some general points about his world view and see how Italy fitted into that world view at that crucial moment.

At the center of his concern, of course, is France itself—a France that has "rolled from the crest of history down to the deepest hollow of the abyss."[10] Those June days saw the nadir of the French state as de Gaulle's account amply shows. He would spend the rest of his life trying to repair this.

Next, and largely off stage in these pages is the cause of these woes: Germany. De Gaulle is clinical, fatalistic, and distanced: "The disproportion between our forces and the Germans' is so great that, barring a miracle, we have no longer any chance of winning in Metropolitan France, or even holding there."[11] Again, the question of Germany and how to manage France's relations with her would be a life-long concern.

Finally there are the Anglo-Saxons—at this point, though, only the British. On June 10 when de Gaulle went to see Reynaud, he found William Bullitt, the American ambassador there: "I supposed that the United States was bringing some encouragement for the future from Washington. But no! He had come to say goodbye. . . . The fact remained that during the supreme days of crisis there would be no American ambassador to the French government."[12] De Gaulle had met Winston Churchill for the first time on June 9. He famously found a kindred spirit, but the Franco-British talks on June 11 were full of misunderstandings and cross purposes, the beginning of a long history of misunderstandings and cross purposes. Even so, the future of France depended on the Anglo-Saxons, and de Gaulle would soon depart for London.

What then of the Italians? We will return later to de Gaulle's broader views of France's "Latin Sister" and to his views of a European concert in general. In June 1940, however, by declaring war on France, Fascist Italy was attempting to "reverse" the traditional and historical positions these nations had held, if not in Europe, at least in the Mediterranean. And, even if this was attempted under the aegis of Germany (and Hitler consistently thwarted Mussolini's ambitions towards France), it still represented a challenge to the idea of France as a great power. For de Gaulle, not only did Fascist Italy have to be defeated, but Italy would have to pay, and in so doing Italy would be put back into her place in the European system. There would be a settling of accounts, but that would depend upon the circumstances surrounding Italy's surrender.

SEPTEMBER 8, 1943

In the early morning of September 8, 1943, General Eisenhower announced the signing of an armistice between Italy and the allies. This is a fateful day in the history of Italy, for it led to the collapse of the state and the disbanding of the army. For some historians, it signifies *"la morte della Patria."* Instead of ending the war in Italy, the conditions on the ground surrounding the armistice prolonged it. As German forces moved in from the north to counter allied armies who had landed in the south, Italy was left to face almost two years of bitter war—and civil war.[13]

French forces were to fight throughout the Italian campaign, and the breakthrough at Monte Cassino was largely due to the French Expeditionary Force. The significance of this day for de Gaulle, however, lay elsewhere. For the events surrounding it raised crucial questions of the central authority of his movement and the role of France in determining the postwar order.

The background to September 8 is Mussolini's fall from power on July 25, 1943, which itself had been triggered by the allied invasion of Sicily. How did de Gaulle view this? First, he delighted in the demise of the jackal: "Mussolini's example is now added to the history of all those who outraged the majesty of France and whom destiny has punished."[14] Second, he stressed that no serious settlement with Italy could be made without France: "The collapse of Italian Fascism may very soon lead to a new settlement of accounts. And it is quite obvious that despite the terrible situation in which our country still finds itself, such a settlement can be neither valid nor lasting without France."[15] Finally, he introduced a new theme, and one that would basically be the cornerstone of his later policies after the liberation of France and as president (1958–1969), of reconciliation rather than revenge, of the ties between the Latin peoples: "since the close proximity, and, to a certain degree, the interdependence of the two great Latin peoples, are still, despite present grievances, the elements on which the reason and hope of Europe do not despair of establishing themselves."[16] In 1943, though, it was the settling of accounts rather than reconciliation that was uppermost in de Gaulle's mind.

The forty five days following Mussolini's fall were crucial, wasted and ended in tragedy. A new Italian government was formed by Marshall Badoglio. Despite the end of Fascism, Italy was still at war and still allied to Germany, of which the King and Badoglio were greatly afraid. They soon opened negotiations with the allies, hoping to strike the best possible deal while keeping the wrathful Germans at bay. On the allied side, the British and the Americans took the lead, despite sharp differences between them, over what to do with Italy. On September 3, 1943, armistice terms were signed, but not announced. The allies had also agreed upon the invasion of mainland Italy, to be spearheaded by an ambitious amphibious landing at Salerno, south of Naples, which would begin on September 8, 1943.

In these same late-summer days, de Gaulle faced two great problems. The first was to consolidate the Free French movement and to solidify his control over it. In practice, this meant empowering the French Committee of Liberation, and, at the same time, out-maneuvering and eventually marginalizing his rival and the darling of the Anglo-Saxons, General Giraud. The second was to make sure that the voice of France would be heard in the councils of the great, particularly since, after Stalingrad, the tide of battle was turning. Italy's surrender would be a first test case, of constructing the new postwar order. The events surrounding September 8 would vex de Gaulle on all counts.

The armistice between Italy and the allies that was proclaimed on September 8 not only came as a complete surprise to General de Gaulle, but, having been approved by Britain, the United States, and the Soviets, left France out altogether. The degree of de Gaulle's chagrin is clear in his memoirs. Already in August the allies had recognized the French Committee of Liberation (in varying degrees: Washington very narrowly, Moscow more broadly, with London in between). Despite previous understandings that France would be a party to the armistice, France was now ignored and the authority of the Committee undermined. On top of that, the dubious role of General Giraud emerged (the Ango-Americans claimed that he had, in fact, been kept *au courant* of the armistice negotiations)—or, in de Gaulle's words: "our allies had invoked if not employed the ridiculous dualism of our government as an alibi for breaking their word."

The crucial issue raised on September 8, though, was France's role in shaping the postwar order, not only in Italy, but in Europe. De Gaulle summed up:

> There could be no doubt: our allies were in agreement to keep us at as great a distance as they could from decisions concerning Italy. We could expect that tomorrow they would make still greater efforts to determine the destiny of Europe without France. But they must be made to realize that France would not tolerate this exclusion and that they could not count on her in the future if they disregarded her now.[17]

September 8 underscores the tremendous difficulties that de Gaulle faced not only in establishing his authority as the leader of the Free French movement, but in impressing his will upon the British and the Americans. Italy was a case in which he would not yield. Mussolini's attack had opened up an account with France; an account that de Gaulle would demand to have settled as the war drew to a close.

SETTLING ACCOUNTS: THE VAL D'AOSTA

De Gaulle began to articulate his view of the future of Franco-Italian relations. His language invariably reflected a long-term perspective favoring reconciliation and Italy's reinsertion in a European concert. At a press conference in October 1945, for example, he set out his basic arguments: (a) Fascism had been an aberration for Italy; (b) a distinction must be made between the responsibilities of the Italians and those of the Germans; (c) Italy is a necessary element in a European system; (d) Italy is France's neighbor, indeed, her cousin; (e) the new democratic political forces in Italy were not at all hostile to France. Therefore reconciliation was possible.[18]

De Gaulle's actual policy towards Italy, however, was rather different. French policy towards Italy between 1944 and 1946 was both rigid and punitive. At the heart of this policy was the view of Italy as a defeated power who must be made to pay. What were the political objectives? According to Pierre Guillen:

> To expunge the humiliation imposed by the Anglo-Americans who, in September 1943, had excluded France from the armistice negotiations and who, since that time, had practically left her out of the conduct of policy towards Italy; to forcibly reinstate a French presence in Italian affairs on an equal footing with the Anglo-Saxons; to obtain a lever with which to press French claims at the time of the peace settlement.[19]

Thus, the narrower Italian policy was linked to the broader goal of reasserting French power in the state system vis-à-vis the allies. The French refused either to recognize Italy's status as a "cobelligerent" or to officially recognize the government. De Gaulle constantly argued that Italy should be treated as a defeated power, and there were conflicts over Italian participation in the Bretton Woods conference, UNRAA relief, and over the treatment of prisoners of war. De Gaulle cut short relations between the French and the Italian resistance movements. Since 1943 French policy had steadily moved to reduce Italian influence in Tunisia and Corsica.

The heart of the matter, though, lay in France's territorial demands upon Italy. And, at that heart of these demands lay the Val d'Aosta. The case of the Val d'Aosta represents a major miscalculation by de Gaulle and it sharply conditioned Italian opinions of him.

The account in de Gaulle's memoirs of his meeting in 1943 with the new Italian foreign minister, Count Sforza, sets the scene. Sforza had come, he told de Gaulle, "to do everything possible to establish that Franco-Italian cooperation for whose lack you and I are paying dearly and which our Europe is going to need more than ever." De Gaulle, for his part, "indicated to Count Sforza how closely I saw eye to eye with him on this crucial point, but after what had happened a reconciliation with Italy could not be made altogether gratuitously, although it was our intention to prepare it as sparingly as possible." What then was the bill to be paid? According to de Gaulle:

> To liquidate the privileges which Italian nationals enjoyed in Tunisia; to award France the cantons of Tende and La Brigue which, although French, had been granted to Italy after the plebiscite of 1860; to rectify the frontier along the passes of Larche, Mont Genevre, Mont Cenis and Little Saint Bernard in order to abolish several awkward encroachments on our territory; to accord Val d'Aosta the right to be what it was—that is a region spiritually French; to demand certain reparations, particularly in regard to warships and commercial vessels: these were the limited but precise advantages which I had determined to assure France.[20]

However limited, but precise these demands may have appeared to de Gaulle, the Italian perspective could not help but be different.

The Val d'Aosta, though perhaps "spiritually" French, had never belonged to France. And, despite a local separatist movement, other more influential intellectuals and resistance leaders were opposed to leaving Italy. In May 1945 French troops entered the Val d'Aosta and French annexationist claims, it seemed, were clear.

The presence of French troops in the Val d'Aosta provoked a severe crisis between de Gaulle and the Americans, who wanted to postpone territorial settlements until after the war. President Truman, in a rage, demanded French withdrawal. He threatened "grave consequences" and the withdrawal of aid. De Gaulle was forced to back down. On June 11, 1945, French forces evacuated the region.[21]

Significant lessons were drawn from the Val d'Aosta affair. For de Gaulle, "To a certain degree, the source of this affair was the United States' desire for hegemony, which they had readily manifested and which I had not failed to discern on every occasion."[22] But even more so, he pointed to the British, who drew parallels between the French behavior in the Val d'Aosta with the more important French interventions in Syria and Lebanon: "For at the same moment, England was preparing her decisive maneuver in the Levant. For London, to inspire Washington to find a source of friction with Paris was a strategic move." Behind the narrow Italian question of the Val d'Aosta, de Gaulle saw the broader problems of American hegemony and French rivalry with a revived British Empire.

The significance for Italy was also great. Sergio Romano has argued that de Gaulle had no real intention of annexing the Val d'Aosta.[23] Rather, he saw it as a diplomatic move to gain a bargaining chip that could be used in future negotiations in order to assert French leadership in Franco-Italian relations. De Gaulle miscalculated greatly, however, as far as Italian public opinion was concerned. The new Italian democratic elite became disillusioned by de Gaulle and risked attacks from the nationalist right. As Ugo La Malfa was to put it, *"Se i giusti diritti dell'Italia democratica saranno rispettati, l'Italia potra' essere un fattore di tranquilita' e di ordine e di civile progresso in Europa. L'umiliazione della democrazia giocherebbe a tutto beneficio del nazionalismo e del fascismo."*[24] There was a second lesson that could be drawn as well, and that was to look to the United States as a patron and protector rather than to France.

De Gaulle had been checked by the Anglo-Americans in the Val d'Aosta. He would have little say in the subsequent reconstruction of Italy, for in despair at the course of French politics, in January 1946 he resigned.

LEGACIES

When de Gaulle returned to power in 1958 what kind of Italy did he find? Firstly, his long term aim of reconciliation between France and Italy had been entirely achieved. Italy was a capitalist democracy in the western camp. Italy was no longer a problem. As Serge Bernstein has observed categorically: *"l'Italie n'occupe pas une place majeure dans les preoccupations de Charles de Gaulle, president de la République."*[25] Throughout his presidency, he rarely mentioned Italy or went beyond the formalities of diplomatic nicety. Either, he was indifferent, or, as Bernstein argues, he was supremely confident in the strength of common ties between Italy and France.

This icing of cordiality lay remarkably over a whole series of rather significant differences of opinion and policy. The Italians were firmly anchored in NATO and the transatlantic alliance. Their vision of Europe was basically federalist. The Italians were not Gaullists and steadily opposed most of what de Gaulle was trying to do internationally. Yet Franco-Italian relations never suffered.

Perhaps de Gaulle really was indifferent. Once he had established a special relationship with Germany, Italy in his imagination occupied only a minor place. To end on a polemical note: After Mussolini's mad attempt to reorder the hierarchy of nations had failed, Italy had been restored to her natural place in the system as the least of the European great powers.

NOTES

1. A general survey of de Gaulle's writings and speeches is now available online through La Fondation Charles de Gaulle at www.charles-de-gaulle.org/.

2. Jean Lacouture, *De Gaulle: The Rebel 1890–1944* (New York: Norton, 1990) and *De Gaulle: The Ruler 1945–1970* (New York: Norton, 1992). See also Johnathan Fenby, *The General: Charles de Gaulle and the France He Saved* (London: Simon and Schuster, 2010).

3. École Française de Rome, *De Gaulle et L'Italie, Collection de l'École Française de Rome, no. 233* (Rome: École Française de Rome, 1997).

4. See the essays by Pierre Milza, Odile Rudelle, and Pierre Guillen in *École Française de Rome*.

5. Charles de Gaulle, *The Complete War Memoirs of Charles De Gaulle* (New York: Simon and Schuster, 1972), 60–61.

6. Denis Mack Smith, *Mussolini's Roman Empire* (Harmondsworth, UK: Penguin, 1976), 219.

7. De Gaulle, 61.

8. Mack Smith, 224.

9. See Odile Rudelle, "L'Italie dans le 'concert européen' du général de Gaulle" in *École Française de Rome*, 29–42.

10. De Gaulle, 60–61.

11. De Gaulle, 53.

12. De Gaulle, 61.

13. For the military background see Douglas Porch, *Hitler's Mediterranean Gamble* (London: Weidenfeld and Nicholson, 2004); for the political and diplomatic dimensions see David W. Ellwood, *Italy 1943–45* (Leicester, UK: Leicester University Press, 1985); for Italy's surrender see Elena Aga Rossi, *A Nation Collapses* (Cambridge: Cambridge University Press, 2000).

14. De Gaulle, 452.

15. De Gaulle, 452–453.

16. De Gaulle, 452–453.

17. De Gaulle, 460–461.

18. Pierre Guillen, "De Gaulle et L'Italie: de la Libération á son départ du pouvoir, 1944–1946" in *École Française de Rome*, 45–64.

19. Cited in Ellwood, 182.

20. De Gaulle, 521–522.

21. Irvin Wall, *The United States and the Making of Postwar France 1945–1954* (Cambridge: Cambridge University Press, 1991), 32.

22. De Gaulle, 875.

23 Sergio Romano, "De Gaulle e i primi governi democratici nell'immediato dopoguerra" in *École Française de Rome*, 21–28.

24 Cited by Romano in *École Française de Rome*, 25–26.

25 Serge Bernstein, "L'Italie dans la pensée et le discours du général de Gaulle de 1958 á 1969" in *École Française de Rome*, 65.

Chapter 6

The Road to Phnom Penh

De Gaulle, the Americans, and Vietnam,
1944–1966

John L. Harper

INTRODUCTION

In August-September 1966, President Charles de Gaulle took a nineteen-day tour of Africa and Asia, culminating in a stop in Polynesia to witness the test of a French nuclear weapon. The trip came within months of his announcement (March 1966) of France's withdrawal from NATO's integrated command, and his much-discussed trip to Moscow (July 1966). A little over a year earlier, the United States had decided to Americanize the ground effort and undertake a costly war of attrition against Viet Cong guerrillas and North Vietnamese Main Force units in South Vietnam. In a brief conversation during a diplomatic reception in Addis Ababa on August 27, de Gaulle signaled a U.S. official that he would be talking about the war during his visit to neutral Cambodia. There should be no question, de Gaulle emphasized, about his affection and admiration for the United States and he extended his warmest wishes to President Lyndon Johnson. "But one must say what one thinks. And the Americans would thank him for it later. It was in their interest and in the interest of all that he would speak."[1]

On September 1, 1966, de Gaulle addressed a crowd of some 200,000 packed into the national sports complex in Phnom Penh. He had often spoken about Vietnam but for the first time he did not mince words about who, in his view, bore the blame for the present, bloody impasse. American "illusions relative to the use of force" had led to an escalation closer and closer to China, increasingly provocative of the USSR, and "more and more threatening to world peace." France's position rested in part, he said, on the example it had set in Algeria: although not defeated, it had decided to put an end to "sterile combat," and had managed to do so without suffering—*"bien au contraire!"*—in terms of power, prestige, and prosperity. America could probably not be defeated in Vietnam, but de Gaulle was dead certain no military solution was possible. Rather, it was necessary to seek peace on the basis of the 1954 Geneva agreements that had ended the first Indo-China war (1946–1954), including the neutralization of the Indo-Chinese peoples. Negotiations, in turn, could not begin without a definite commitment by the United States to withdraw its forces within a reasonable period. De Gaulle was under no illusions, he said, that the time was ripe for such a solution. (Although he did not say so, he believed the opportunity had been missed several times and would not come soon again.) Still, it was necessary to affirm that there was no alternative, "save to condemn the world to ever greater misfortunes." France spoke, finally, not only in the name of "its own experience and disinterestedness" but because of its "exceptional friendship" for America. In contrast to the argument often heard in Washington (although infrequently elsewhere) that U.S. standing and credibility would suffer crippling blows were America to withdraw without defeating the Communists, de Gaulle expressed his conviction that given American wealth, power, and influence, a negotiated settlement would contain nothing that "could definitively wound the pride, contradict the ideals, and harm the interests" of the United States.[2]

As de Gaulle had surely anticipated, the Americans did not believe his pronouncement contained sound advice nor did they consider it a friendly gesture—quite the opposite. Secretary of State Dean Rusk was particularly incensed because de Gaulle had spoken only days after a confidential State Department request to Paris to tell the Cambodian and North Vietnamese governments that the United States sincerely wished to end the war. Undersecretary of State for Political Affairs Averell Harriman thought the speech had made Hanoi more intransigent.[3] U.S. ambassador to Paris, Charles Bohlen (a pessimist on Franco-American relations but not, like Rusk, a visceral anti-Gaullist), called de Gaulle's words "a further example of his ignoring facts in favor of his favorite position." He found it "extraordinary that an alleged ally of the United States would present right on the spot within a few kilometers of the battle line so erroneous a picture of cause and effect. De Gaulle appears to heap all the blame for the situation, its origins and development in Indochina, on the United States explicitly. . . . He makes no mention of Communism as a factor and consequently his comparison with the French in Algeria is erroneous and misleading."[4]

Coming in the context of de Gaulle's other moves, it was (and is) easy to conclude that the speech was part of what had become an across-the-board campaign to undermine the U.S. world position. In particular, de Gaulle (despite assertions to the contrary) seemed to be trying to undermine U.S. prestige and influence in the Third World and position France to benefit from what a contemporary commentator called "Gulliver's troubles."[5] De Gaulle, according to this view, may well have welcomed America's prodigious waste of blood and treasure in Vietnam because, by weakening the United States, the war would accelerate a transition to the kind of multipolar international system de Gaulle favored. Otherwise, why did he not give concrete diplomatic (no one expected military) assistance to the Americans, or at least remain silent, rather than rubbing salt in their wounds? And perhaps de Gaulle was driven not just by ambition but *Schadenfueude* and resentment. After all, the French had failed to hold Indo-China and it would be only human to take a certain pleasure and satisfaction in watching the Americans do the same. De Gaulle, moreover, could hardly have forgotten that the United States had recently joined with the Atlanticist wing of the German CDU to try to foil his European plans.

Was the American analysis correct, if not all at least in part? What *were* de Gaulle's motives in denouncing U.S. policy while apparently declining to facilitate U.S. diplomatic efforts? How did he arrive at his views and why did he finally express them with brutal frankness? Why did the Americans reject de Gaulle's advice and how did the Vietnam question affect Franco-American relations? What does the episode say about his basic view of the United States? The story begins in 1944.

LEARNING THE HARD WAY:
DE GAULLE AND INDOCHINA, 1944–1954

"From 1940 to 1945," Jean Lacouture observes, "just as Churchill was the guardian of the isle, he [de Gaulle] was the guardian of the integrity of the Empire."[6] Or to paraphrase the British statesman, de Gaulle did not become leader of French resistance to the Axis (and in 1944 head of the GPRF—the Provisional Government of the French Republic) to preside over the liquidation of France's overseas possessions. It was not simply a question of patriotic sentiment and economic interest linked to the colonies (although both counted). France's position as a great power had depended to a considerable degree on the resources and strong-points of the empire. In 1940–1945, securing the empire provided legitimacy for the Free French cause as well as a base of operations for the liberation of France itself. This was true first of all of Africa. "It was in Africa," de Gaulle wrote, "that we French had to resume the struggle."[7] At the same time, de Gaulle and his entourage were not blind to the political-psychological fallout of the 1940 débacle and the fact that France would emerge from the war with its control over parts of the empire seriously undermined[8]. Even if they had been, pressure for decolonization from the American benefactor would have obliged them to look for new arrangements that accommodated local demands for autonomy. At the Brazzaville conference (January 30–February 8, 1944) attended by colonial officials, de Gaulle outlined his vision of an imperial federation (later called "union") in which the citizens of the colonies would elect assemblies and enjoy a limited degree of self-rule, with the mother country in control of finance, foreign policy, and defense.[9] France's Indochinese colonies (Laos and Cambodia; and Cochinchina, Annam, and Tonkin, making up historic Vietnam), ruled by a Vichy governor general after 1940, were less accessible to Free French influence than Africa, and of limited importance in the war to win back the *métropole*. But they were the key to France's position as an Asian power, and de Gaulle had no intention of allowing them to fall into foreign hands. He recalled that Indochina had seemed "like a great crippled ship that I could only rescue after having at length collected the means to save it. Watching it drift off into the mist, I swore to myself that one day I would bring it back."[10]

The opportunity appeared to have arrived in early-to-mid 1945. President Franklin Roosevelt believed France had "milked" Indochina for decades and deserved to lose it, as well as its bases at New Caledonia, Bizerte, and Dakar. But FDR's policy of hostility toward France and de Gaulle's pretensions to lead it was overtaken by events. Roosevelt had gradually given in to the State Department and British argument that France must be strengthened and given a place on the United Nations Security Council. He resisted the notion that France would retain Indochina, but his idea of creating a U.N. trusteeship there under a weak China looked increasingly impractical. An important turning point occurred on March 9, 1945. Fearing a U.S. attempt to occupy Indochina, the Japanese toppled the Vichy government and assumed control. With some of the local French forces fighting the Japanese, FDR conceded: "Well, if we can get the proper pledge from France to assume for herself the obligations of a trustee, then I would agree to France retaining these colonies" for the time-being.[11] On March 24, 1944, de Gaulle called for resistance to Japan and a federal state of the five Indochinese colonies within a French Union. In June, President Harry Truman endorsed the State Department–British view that French sovereignty should be recognized. At Potsdam in July it was agreed that the Chinese would take the Japanese surrender north of the 16th parallel and the British in southern Vietnam.

But de Gaulle's plans to put himself at the helm of the wayward vessel faced a series of insuperable obstacles. When ousting Vichy, the Japanese had granted full independence to Laos, Cambodia, and a united Vietnam. The subsequent French offer (granting mere autonomy and perpetuating the colonial-era division of Vietnam into three parts) was unacceptable to Vietnamese nationalists of all stripes. War with Japan and French weakness on the ground allowed Ho Chi Minh, charismatic head of the Viet Minh (Vietnam Independence League), to strengthen his position in Tonkin (capital, Hanoi) with the assistance of the American O.S.S. By the time Japan's surrender (August 1945) permitted de Gaulle to dispatch his hand-picked representatives, Admiral Georges Thierry d'Argenlieu (high commissioner) and General Phillipe Leclerc (commander of a French expeditionary force of 70,000), Ho had declared (September 2, 1945) an independent Democratic Republic of Vietnam. De Gaulle's plan to place the exiled Duy Tan on the throne of a united Vietnam collapsed when the former boy emperor died in a plane crash in Chad in December 1945. De Gaulle himself resigned as head of the GPRF in January 1946.

De Gaulle's September 1945 instructions to d'Argenlieu and Leclerc indicate that he had wanted to consolidate control over Cochinchina (capital, Saigon) where French influence was strongest and then negotiate an agreement with the northern forces, without haste, and from a position of military strength. He was absolutely determined to prevent American or British meddling in French colonial affairs of the kind that had occurred in the war. (He suspected British intelligence had killed Duy Tan, but later admitted the British had placed no barriers to France's return to southern Vietnam.)[12] As a spectator after January 1946, he used his influence (on d'Argenlieu, for example) to discourage concessions to the Viet Minh. De Gaulle and (after 1947) the RPF were strong supporters of the anti-Communist war that began with d'Argenlieu's shelling of Hanoi in November 1946. "France must stay in Indochina," he declared in November 1949. "She must stay there for Indochina." In April 1951, he declared that "the war in which we're engaged in Indochina and here [at home] is the war for liberty." As late as mid-May 1954, after the fall of Dien Bien Phu, he called for the dispatch of four divisions stationed in Germany to hold the French position in Laos, Cambodia, and Cochinchina.[13]

In reality, and despite the contradictions in his position, he had seen the writing on the wall. "The Indochina affair is virtually over. . . . It's understood that France won't keep Indochina, that she won't possess it anymore." He spoke thus on March 10, 1954, three days before the Viet Minh occupied the high ground around Dien Bien Phu, dooming the French position. In April, he insisted that the now fully-independent states of Indochina must remain in some way associated with the Union. But he also said France "must try to end the war," and welcomed the Geneva conference.[14] Certainly, he had given up hope of holding northern Vietnam, even in the event of a last-minute U.S. and British intervention (requested by the Laniel government but ultimately turned down by Washington).[15] The turning point in the war, he reflected in May 1954, had been the Chinese Communist victory in 1949, allowing the junction of the Viet Minh and Chinese armies and forcing the French to abandon northern Tonkin. After 1950 (and as recent histories attest), the Chinese were able to provide essential operational and logistical support to the Viet Minh.[16] French public support for the war had faded by 1952–1953.

De Gaulle and most of the former RPF (now URAS) members of parliament supported the Geneva agreements negotiated by the Pierre Mendès–France government. The agreements prohibited independent Laos, Cambodia, and Vietnam from hosting foreign troops or joining alliances, divided Vietnam temporarily at the 17th parallel, and called for elections to create a single government in 1956. In the event, Washington sponsored a southern Republic of Vietnam (RVN) and encouraged its Saigon-based government not to feel bound by the elections provision.[17] Although initially divided, the Eisenhower administration decided it had found an effective anti-Communist nationalist in Ngo Dinh Diem.[18] Thanks in part to generous U.S. aid, Diem had some success in consolidating his position and stabilizing the economy in 1955–1958. French political influence sharply declined (the last French troops left in 1956), although France retained a substantial cultural and economic presence in Vietnam.

De Gaulle's later stance was undoubtedly influenced by the feeling that the Americans were interlopers who had elbowed their way into southern Vietnam and usurped France's rightful position. In opposing the U.S. presence, he hoped to salvage something of France's historic role. At the same time, he appears to have drawn several more objective lessons from the war that underlay his analysis of the second Indochina conflict that began in 1958–1959. While he tended to blame the Paris "regime des parties" for mismanaging the war, he called it "an incredibly difficult cause," implying the situation might well have been beyond his powers to save if he had remained in power.[19] As he put it to President John Kennedy in 1961: Southeast Asia was simply "a bad terrain militarily, politically, and psychologically to fight a war." France's situation "had become worse as more and more outside effort was poured in."[20] A second lesson concerned China and its relations with Vietnam. Chinese help had guaranteed Communist success, and one could not have defeated the Viet Minh without dealing effectively with their northern neighbor. By the same token, the PRC (together with the USSR) had pressured the North Vietnamese into accepting a compromise settlement in

1954. This incurred North Vietnamese resentment, especially after the 1956 elections did not take place. While North Vietnam was dependent on China *in wartime,* nothing in the history of their relations suggested Hanoi wished to be Beijing's satellite, and an independent Vietnam might be a barrier to Chinese expansion.

There followed a third, closely-related lesson: nationalism was everywhere a growing force, "even in communism." Communism, de Gaulle said in 1954, "survives to the extent that it is nationalism."[21] Nationalism was Ho's ace card in the hole. A final lesson had to do with the Americans. Although the United States had heavily subsidized the war, it had not intervened to prevent a French defeat. More strikingly to de Gaulle, the Americans had not taken the Korean war to China when they might have done so to their advantage. "If America in 1951," he said on more than one occasion, "had listened to MacArthur, she would have won the Asian war because she was the only one then with atomic bombs."[22] And, he was probably thinking, she would have changed the course of the Indochina war.) "If you're a colossus you make war, or else you sit in an armchair to smoke a pipe and watch television." The Americans, de Gaulle said (echoing Napoleon on the English), were Carthaginians, not Romans, a commercial rather than a warrior people.[23] If they were ever to find themselves in a situation where the basic choice was either to accept the loss of South Vietnam or take the war to China, he probably surmised, the Americans would shrink before the latter prospect. And if they did not, they would be undertaking a major war for the sake of a rotten and artificial creation. This was more or less the situation he saw the Americans facing in 1963–1964.

THE SHOE ON THE OTHER FOOT

In 1957–1958, elements of the Viet Minh who had gone underground launched an armed struggle against the RVN. Hounded by government forces, the Viet Minh (called "Viet Cong"—Vietnamese Communists—by the South Vietnamese) assassinated village officials and carried out hit-and-run attacks. Having decided to resume the struggle more or less on their own, the southern-based Communists lobbied the north for support. Many in Hanoi were reluctant to risk a major conflict. With reason, however, they felt cheated by Geneva. Fearing Diem would grow stronger with time, Hanoi approved a "people's war" in January 1959. The following year, it infiltrated a 10,000-strong cadre into the south and sponsored a multi-party (although Communist-controlled) political organization committed to reunification, the National Liberation Front (NLF). Moscow and Beijing were even more skeptical than Hanoi of the chances of winning and warned the North Vietnamese against an "insurrectionist" strategy. But as the anti-RVN campaign gained momentum, Beijing threw its weight behind the struggle. Saigon's heavy-handed response, including the forced transfer of peasants to new villages and the brutal suppression of non-Communist opposition groups, incurred hatred of the regime and won support for the NLF.[24]

Kennedy had partially followed de Gaulle's advice, sending U.S. advisers rather than (as Robert McNamara had counseled in 1961) combat troops. As conditions grew problematic, U.S. officials generally retained their faith in victory, pointing to the success in parts of South Vietnam of a system of "strategic hamlets" administered by Diem's brother, Ngo Dinh Nhu. But Viet Cong strength increased, and the political situation precipitated in May 1963 with the start of Buddhist and student protests against Diem's authoritarian behavior. In August 1963, Nhu's Special Forces carried out brutal raids against the pagodas, provoking international outrage and disgust. The Americans now faced the choice of a collapsing South Vietnamese state and war effort, or deeper U.S. involvement. They were divided on the question of whether to encourage a coup by ARVN generals or to sink or swim with the Ngos.[25] There was also a third possibility much in the air in late summer 1963. Nhu made little secret of his animus toward America's invasive presence and interest in a negotiated settlement. Saigon might do a deal with the Communists and invite the Americans to leave.

De Gaulle's diplomacy aimed, in effect, to convince the parties that some version of this third possibility was preferable for all concerned. On August 29, 1963, his statement to the cabinet on Vietnam was given verbatim to the press. It spoke of a country "independent of outside influences, in internal peace and unity, and in concord with its neighbors." France wanted such a result for "all of Vietnam" and was ready to assist. Essentially, de Gaulle was calling for a return to the Geneva formula: a neutral, unified Vietnam, with no foreign troops on its soil. Although he did not say so ("a certain blurring of categories," the historian Frederik Logevall observes, "was necessary to get negotiations started"), he had in mind the neutralization of South Vietnam as a first step, followed eventually by reunification with the north.[26]

For Paris, the situation was both urgent and ripe for a solution. It was urgent because the Americans, near the end of their tether with the Ngos, were conspiring to remove them in favor of generals opposed to negotiation. The French ambassador in Saigon, Roger Lalouette (with de Gaulle's blessing he had been secretly encouraging Nhu to negotiate with the Communists), defended the government to U.S. ambassador Henry Cabot Lodge the day after de Gaulle's statement, and advised against a coup.[27] It was ripe for a solution because the South could not cope with the Communists unless the

Americans took on the North and China directly. The North was willing to compromise to remove the Americans and avoid a protracted war, and had signaled its interest in a neutral South Vietnam presided over by a coalition government.[28] The USSR, a player in any negotiations, had discouraged the North Vietnamese from challenging the Americans and (like Hanoi itself) did not want to see them under Chinese influence. Khrushchev had gone along with the neutralization of Laos in 1962 and was interested above all in détente with the United States. The Chinese were more problematical partners. They were determined to challenge Moscow as the main sponsor of Third World revolutions. But as both de Gaulle and Foreign Minister Maurice Couve de Murville would argue to U.S. officials, China was still fundamentally weak, preoccupied with internal consolidation, and prepared to pay a price to avoid a clash with the United States. For France itself, the de Gaulle solution would build on the Algerian success, enhancing worldwide French prestige and influence. If Washington rejected his idea, de Gaulle was prepared to wait. Sooner or later the *Americans* would see the writing on the wall.[29] The U.S. reaction to de Gaulle's statement combined incomprehension, exasperation, and near-desperation. What, the Americans asked, did de Gaulle mean? A Laos-like solution? Didn't he see that fighting hadn't stopped in Laos and the Communists were gaining? The French answers to these questions were unconvincing unless one accepted their premises that a united Communist Vietnam would be anti-Chinese, and that there was no military solution. Much like the French in 1944–1954, the Americans insisted on negotiating from a position of strength, if at all, thought the war was an essential part of a broader anti-Communist struggle, and bristled when outsiders meddled in their business. (National security adviser McGeorge Bundy referred to the French president as "Nosey Charlie.")[30] Given recent events—the U.S-French clashes over the MLF, British common market membership, and the Franco-German treaty—the Americans suspected de Gaulle was trying to pay them back or undermine their position. Although they made a tactical decision to treat de Gaulle with kid gloves (a polemical or punitive attitude, they decided, would only serve his purposes,[31] they were deeply irritated. Above all, they feared, de Gaulle was poisoning the morale of the South Vietnamese army and population. The day before the Lalouette-Lodge conversation, Kennedy had given the green light to a coup by ARVN generals. The generals had backed off but then moved in early November, ousting (and killing) the Ngos, with American backing. One of their motives was to prevent a deal with the North, and the coup put an end to the French bid to use Diem and Nhu to break the impasse in Vietnam.

De Gaulle's next diplomatic bombshell came in January 1964: French recognition of the PRC. One of the reasons was better to ascertain Chinese thinking on Vietnam and engage Beijing in his "new Geneva" initiative. Unfortunately, the context and timing were even less propitious than in the previous August, at least from the point of view of Washington. It requires a considerable leap of faith to believe Kennedy would have withdrawn U.S. forces from Vietnam regardless of political-military conditions, and/or pursued neutralization. But he was a more seasoned international operator than Johnson, having shown his mettle in Cuba and Berlin. Johnson, although tortured by doubts about the war, was firmly in the grip of the "iron law" of American politics: your opponent will make you pay if you look weak. Pressed by Rusk, McNamara, and Bundy, he decided (while wanting to avoid a wider war before the November elections) to keep the military pressure on Hanoi and reject any step that might expose himself to Republican censure.[32] As in August 1963, de Gaulle's move provoked dismay because it might undermine (perhaps that was de Gaulle's aim?) the precarious situation in Saigon. Washington welcomed a second coup in January 1964 by hard-line generals who suspected that the November coup-plotters—encouraged by de Gaulle's opening to China—were themselves considering a deal with the North! LBJ told Lodge that his mission was "precisely for the purpose of knocking down the idea of neutralization whenever it rears its ugly head, and on this point I think that nothing is more important than to stop neutralist talk wherever we can by whatever means we can."[33] Privately, there were signs of de Gaulle's own exasperation. In January 1964, he remarked to information minister Alain Peyrefitte: "If the Americans are not too stupid they will put an end to this absurd Vietnam war."[34] But he stuck to his guns and waited for the Americans to come around to what he saw as the unassailable logic of his position. In April 1964, when Washington ordered Bohlen to solicit a public statement from the French to the effect that, while favoring neutralization they did not think it applied at the present moment, de Gaulle refused. According to Bohlen:

> De Gaulle was courteous and affable throughout . . . but showed no sign whatsoever of changing his attitude. It seems to me that what this adds up to is his firm belief that the course we are on, i.e., supporting the Vietnamese Government, is one that will only end in failure and that the best policy for the United States was to opt for an immediate policy of neutralization. The only other alternative he could see would be one in which the United States would enlarge the war by an attack on North Vietnam and probably China.[35]

The contemporaneous position of the Foreign Ministry was somewhat more nuanced, assuring the Americans that France opposed a Communist South Vietnam. But, if, as Couve told Rusk shortly after the Bohlen–de Gaulle meeting, the United States could not win it was better off taking its chances with a neutralized South Vietnam.[36] De Gaulle was not without American converts and supporters. Walter Lippmann and the editorial page of the *New York Times* supported a negotiated settlement along the lines of Geneva. The DCM in Saigon, David Nes, expressed agreement with de Gaulle's analysis (i.e., the choice was between failure and escalation), as did Undersecretary of State George Ball. In a step reminiscent of Comintern practice (and ignoring Bohlen's advice that it would be useless to try to change de Gaulle's mind), LBJ sent in-house dissenter Ball to Paris in June 1964 to repeat the White House line. Ball dutifully performed his mission, but the meeting served only to reveal the closeness of Ball's real views to de Gaulle's.[37] De Gaulle received a boost in mid-1964 when U.N. Secretary General U Thant called for a reconvening of the Geneva conference to negotiate peace in Southeast Asia. In a July 23, 1964, press conference de Gaulle repeated that there was no military solution. Of course, some imagined that the Americans might seek one by pursuing the war as far north as necessary. But it was hard to admit that they wanted "to take on the enormous adventure of a generalized conflict." Echoing Thant (and adding more specifics than previously), de Gaulle called for a reconvening of Geneva without prior conditions. The settlement would be based on the neutrality of Laos, Cambodia and Vietnam, and the non-engagement of France, China, the USSR, and the United States.[38] U.S. policy was ineluctably moving in a different direction. Johnson's reaction to de Gaulle's statement was that "We do not believe in conferences called to ratify terror, so our policy is unchanged."[39] In May, Rusk, McNamara, and Bundy recommended that if North Vietnam failed to heed warnings to end the war, the United States should "use selected and carefully graduated military force against" it. LBJ followed the advice, relaying warnings to Hanoi through a Canadian diplomat and taking advantage of an attack on a U.S. destroyer in the Gulf of Tonkin in August to bomb North Vietnam and obtain a sweeping Congressional mandate authorizing him to take whatever steps he considered necessary to protect U.S. lives in Southeast Asia.[40] In early 1965, the French tried again to head off a major escalation. On February 19, Couve informed Johnson at the White House that (according to the Chinese ambassador to Paris), Beijing was ready to go back to the 1954 agreement "as a basis for negotiations." One could not predict what kind of government would emerge in South Vietnam. This "was a risk which one would probably have to take." The Russians, he added, "were a moderating element" and had the same position as the French.[41] That China might compromise to avoid a U.S. escalation that could involve it in the fighting was also suggested by Mao's conciliatory interview in January 1965 to the American journalist Edgar Snow, in which he suggested Chinese forces would remain at home.[42] The French were wasting their breath, as they themselves suspected.[43] The window of opportunity, if there had ever been one, was quickly closing. Among other negative developments, Paris must have seen, was that Moscow was becoming part of the problem rather than the solution. The post-Khrushchev leadership was less interested in détente and more inclined to back the Vietnamese comrades. The Americans brazenly bombed Hanoi during the visit of premier Aleksei Kosygin in February and the USSR joined China as an indispensable backer of North Vietnam in 1965. Meanwhile, in what became known as the "fork in the road memo" (January 27, 1965), Bundy and McNamara had warned Johnson that the current "essentially passive role" of the United States could "only lead to eventual defeat and an invitation to get out under humiliating circumstances." The choice was to use U.S. power to try to change Communist policy and shore up South Vietnam, or else negotiate a withdrawal. To mention the latter option was to reject it. Washington used the Viet Cong raid on the airfield and barracks at Pleiku on February 6, killing eight U.S. advisers, as the pretext for a major escalation. Operation "Rolling Thunder," the systematic bombing of the North, began in March. The decision for large U.S. ground forces followed in July 1965.

CONCLUSION

The 1965 escalation ended hopes for an early return to Geneva and provoked anger and resignation. It reinforced de Gaulle's determination to pursue a policy independent of the United States. In March he told his cabinet that his efforts had failed and the war would go on indefinitely. In April 1965, he said, "If the United States does not decide now to withdraw from Vietnam, the war will last ten years [a prediction accurate down to the month]. And the war will never end without the Americans losing face [another accurate prediction], unlike the Algerian war, which ended with France's honor intact." He continued to talk to the Americans about Vietnam and went to considerable lengths to maintain contacts with China, North Vietnam, and the NLF (using André Malraux, Jean Chauvel, and his old envoy to Hanoi, Jean Sainteny, as his eyes and ears, and carrying on a correspondence with Ho) in preparation for possible negotiations.[44] For their part, the Americans continued to be vexed and perplexed by the French stand which was now hard for them to separate from the dramatic (presumably anti-American) démarche on NATO and the trip to the USSR. Indeed, when de Gaulle announced (February 21, 1966) that France would leave NATO's integrated command, one of the reasons he cited (although not the first one) was that the U.S. escalation in Vietnam might produce "a general conflagration" into which France, as a member of the command and a base of NATO operations, would be drawn against its will.[45]

On August 23, 1966, Rusk wrote Couve de Murville asking him to pass a message to the Cambodians and North Vietnamese: "We have repeatedly stated our intention to withdraw once this [North Vietnamese] interference is at an end. This intention is categorical. . . . It is of course always possible that the result might be achieved simply by announced reciprocal actions, made known between Hanoi and ourselves through secret channels."[46] France's answer to this request was the Phnom Penh address, the equivalent of a slap in the face.

Was de Gaulle deliberately withholding French help out of spite and/or in hopes the Americans would sink further into the Vietnam quagmire? No doubt a certain weakening of the U.S. world position suited his purposes, and if Vietnam provided another argument for independence from NATO so much the better. No doubt there was also an element of "it serves them right" satisfaction in saying no to the U.S. request. After all, the Americans had refused to be helped in 1963–1964 when conditions for a compromise were riper and they would have had less to lose. That said, de Gaulle's main motives around the time of Phnom Penh were rather different. After all, there was not much de Gaulle could do to undermine the Americans that they were not already doing to themselves. If he had wanted them to throw away their energies in Vietnam he would have been giving them a different kind of advice.

One motive (although not necessarily the most important) was surely further to consolidate France's post-Algeria position as a champion of Third World nationalism and influential friend of Indochina. Another was real concern about the possibility of war between the United States and China (and possibly the USSR) that might involve France, and even if it did not, seriously dissipate U.S. strength. As in 1950–1954, the Chinese were providing indispensable aid to the North Vietnamese. (At the height of their involvement, in 1967, the Chinese had 170,000 engineering and anti-aircraft personnel in North Vietnam, permitting Hanoi to cover its rear and operate on a large scale in the South.) According to de Gaulle's basic analysis, the Americans would either have to take the war further and further north or else impose limits on themselves to avoid war with China and, in so doing, condemn themselves to stalemate or defeat in the south. The memory of Korea and his view of the United States *cum* Carthage suggested (accurately) that they would adopt the latter course. But the choice was still open and he probably knew that the U.S. military was eager to take the war to the north. Finally, and regardless of Rusk's request, de Gaulle could see that the Americans were not ready for negotiations. They were in the middle of a major effort and it was inconceivable that they would reverse course and commit themselves to withdrawal before seeing the results. The very language of Rusk's message suggested they were not serious. Calling the Communist presence in the south "interference" indicated they were clinging to old categories about Vietnam.

Although he does not say so explicitly, de Gaulle must have been struck frequently by the similarities between the American and French situations. His remarkable "clairvoyance" consisted basically of remembering what had already happened to France in Indochina. He probably had doubts all along as to whether the Americans would listen to outside advice, or thank him for giving it. After all, France had not. As was only human, the Americans would have to learn the hard way, like the French. (In fact, they began to come around to de Gaulle's position after the February 1968 Tet offensive.) But this did not absolve him from the responsibility of speaking frankly. And although he was fond of saying that *"un état digne de ce nom n'a pas d'ami,"*[47] he seems to have looked on the United States (perhaps because it was itself not really a state?) as an exception to the rule. On the contrary, he believed the "exceptional friendship" between the two countries required confronting the Americans with reality rather than remaining silent or simply repeating to them the "truth" that they wanted to be told.

NOTES

1. Korry, Embassy in Ethiopia, to Department of State (hereafter DOS), Aug. 27, 1966, *Foreign Relations of the United States (FRUS),* 1964–1968, 12:129.

2. De Gaulle, Phnom Penh speech, Sept. 1, 1966, in *Discours et Messages,* Vol. 5 (Plon: Paris, 1970–71), 74–78. (All translations by the author.)

3. On this point see Charles G. Cogan, "'How Fuzzy Can One Be?' The American Reaction to de Gaulle's Proposal for the Neutralization of (South) Vietnam" in Lloyd C. Gardner and Ted Gittinger, *The Search for Peace in Vietnam, 1964–1968* (College Station: Texas A&M University Press, 2004), 158.

4. Bohlen to DOS, Sept. 1, 1966, *FRUS,* 1964–1968, 12:130–31. On Bohlen's more general views, see his *Witness to History* (New York: Norton, 1973), chap. 28.

5. Stanley Hoffman, *Gulliver's Troubles* (New York: McGraw Hill, 1968).

6. Jean Lacouture, *De Gaulle: Le Rebelle* (Paris: Editions du Seuil, 1984), 749–53.

7. *Ibid.,* 429, quoting de Gaulle's war memoirs.

8. He said at the Brazzaville conference that "beneath the action of the psychic forces it [the war] has everywhere unleashed, every population looks ahead and questions itself as to its destiny!" De Gaulle, *War Memoirs, Unity* (New York: Carroll & Graf, 1998), 512.

9. Jean Lacouture, *De Gaulle: Le Rebelle,* 749–53.

10. Statements quoted in J.-R. Tournoux, *La Tragedie du General* (Paris: Plon, 1967), 113–14.

11. FDR quoted in Stein Tonnesson, "Franklin Roosevelt, Trusteeship, and Indochina: A Reassessment," in Mark Atwood Lawrence and Frederik Logevall, eds., *The First Vietnam War* (Cambridge: Harvard University Press, 2007), 67.

12. *Ibid.*, 447, *Le Rebelle*, quoting de Gaulle's war memoirs.

13. On instructions, see de Gaulle's press conference, June 30, 1955, *Discours et Messages*, 640–41. On his suspicions of the British role in the plane crash, see Lacouture, *De Gaulle: Le Politique*, 168.

14. See de Gaulle press conference, Apr. 7, 1954, *Discours et Messages*, 614. Under U.S. pressure Paris had finally ceded full independence in Apr. 1954.

15. In the press conference cited in the previous note, de Gaulle said only that any foreign force must be under French command. He did not comment on the possibility of a U.S. air operation, under discussion at the time. The Eisenhower administration, while favoring an intervention, declined to do so without explicit Congressional approval. Skeptical Congressional leaders, in turn, insisted that the British take part in any operation. London was adamantly opposed, and this condition doomed the possibility of an attempt to save Dien Bien Phu.

16. *Ibid.*, 167, 176–78. See also chapter 5, "China and the First Indochina War" in Chen Jian, *Mao's China in the Cold War* (Chapel Hill: University of North Carolina Press, 2001).

17. The population of northern Vietnam was 13 million; that of Vietnam south of the 17th parallel, 9 million.

18. In 1955, when Diem (premier of the government of absentee Emperor Bao Dai) was challenged for control of Saigon by the armed religious sects, the Hoa Hao and the Cao Dai, and the criminal organization, Binh Xuyen, the U.S. Ambassador in Saigon, General Lawton Collins, took the position that Diem should be replaced. Diem was strongly supported by the Dulles brothers and Col. Edward Lansdale, the counter-insurgency specialist who advised the Saigon government. With U.S. Support, Diem and the army managed to defeat the threat and temporarily silence the critics. In Oct. 1955, Diem organized a referendum (in which he received 98 percent of the votes) to oust Bao Dai and create a republic. See Herring, 51–56. On the transition from French to U.S. influence see also, Mark A. Lawrence, *Assuming the Burden: Europe and the American Commitment to War in Vietnam* (Berkeley: University of California Press, 2005); Kathryn C. Statler, *Replacing France: The Origins of American Intervention in Vietnam* (Lexington: University Press of Kentucky, 2007); Jessica M. Chapman, "Staging Democracy: South Vietnam's 1955 Referendum to Depose Bao Dai," *Diplomatic History*, vol. 30, no. 4 (Sept. 2006), 671–703.

19. De Gaulle press conference, June 30, 1955, *Discours et Message*, 640.

20. De Gaulle-Kennedy conversation in Paris, June 2, 1961, *FRUS*, 1961–1963, 13:663.

21. March 10, 1954 remarks quoted in Tournoux, 167.

22. This was not strictly accurate because the PRC's ally, the USSR, although not a direct participant, also had the bomb. See de Gaulle press conference, Apr. 7, 1954, *Discours et Messages*, 605. See also Mar. 10, 1954 remarks quoted in Tournoux, 165.

23. *Ibid.*, 165.

24. On events in Vietnam, see *ibid.,* 180–183; Herring, 66–67.

25. The anti-Diem faction in Washington was spearheaded by State Department officials Averell Harriman and Roger Hilsman, and Michael Forrestal of the NSC staff. In Saigon, Henry Cabot Lodge (appointed ambassador in August 1963) energetically supported the coup and was instrumental in convincing Kennedy to go along. Vice President Johnson feared the consequences of a coup and thought it wiser to stick with Diem. Also opposed to a coup were the CIA station chief in Saigon, John Richardson (recalled in Oct. at Lodge's request) and the head of the U.S. military mission, Gen. Paul Harkins. McNamara and Gen. Maxwell Taylor (at this point Chairman of the JCS) were skeptical but eventually took the position that, while not actively encouraged, a coup should not be thwarted by the United States For Kennedy's statement, see minutes of White House meeting, Oct. 29, 1963, *FRUS,* 1961–63, 4: doc. 235.

26. De Gaulle quoted in Frederik Logevall, *Choosing War* (Berkeley: University of California Press, 1999), 2. See also *ibid.,* 104.

27. On Lalouette, see Ellen Hammer, *A Death in November: America in Vietnam, 1963* (New York: E.P. Dutton, 1987), 224–33. Memo of conversation between Lalouette and Lodge, Aug. 30, 1963, *FRUS,* 1961–1963, 4: 58–59.

28. See Logevall, 9, 12.

29. *Ibid.,* 14–15, 176.

30. See Bundy to Kennedy, Sept. 1, 1963, *FRUS,* 1961–1963, 4: 81.

31. On this point see memo cited in previous note. See also Bohlen, *Witness to History,* chap. 28.

32. By the same token, he hoped to portray his opponent Barry Goldwater as the warmonger and would famously tell the public during the campaign, "We still seek no wider war."

33. Johnson to Lodge, Mar. 20, 1964, *FRUS,* 1964–1968, 1: 185.

34. On de Gaulle's public and private statements, see Logevall's detailed account in *Choosing War,* 1–16, 95–107.

35. Bohlen to DOS, Apr. 2, 1964, reporting on his 45-min. conversation, *FRUS.,* 1964–1968, 1: 219.

36. Memo of conversation at the SEATO conference in Manila, Apr. 12, 1963, *ibid.,* 234–36. See also Rusk to Lodge, Feb. 29, 1964, reporting the views of French ambassador to Washington Hervé Alphand, *ibid.,* 107–8.

37. See Nes to Lodge, Feb. 17, 1964, *ibid.,* 90–92. On Ball and de Gaulle, see Logevall, 175–76.

38. De Gaulle press conference, July 23, 1964, *Discours et Messages,* 236–37.

39. Quoted in Logevall, 188.

40. A first attack by a North Vietnamese patrol boat occurred on August 2, 1964, in what North Vietnam considered its territorial waters. A reported attack on another destroyer on Aug. 4, much further from the coast, probably never occurred, the report being the result of a nervous reaction in difficult weather conditions by the destroyer's crew. Nonetheless, it was the alleged second attack that triggered Washington's response. For a lucid account of the incident (s), see Daniel Ellsberg, *Secrets: A*

Memoir of Vietnam and the Pentagon Papers (New York: Penguin, 2002), chap. 1. Acting through the Canadian diplomat Blair Seaborn, Washington had secretly warned Hanoi in June that U.S. public and official patience with North Vietnamese "aggression" against South Vietnam was "growing extremely thin," and that if the conflict escalated North Vietnam itself would suffer the "greatest devastation." On the Seaborn mission, see Ellsberg, 17.

41. See memo of conversation, Feb. 19, 1965, *FRUS, 1964–1968*, 82–87.

42. To Snow, whom he sometimes used as a conduit for conciliatory signals to the United States, Mao said, *"China's armies would not go beyond her borders to fight. That was clear enough. Only if the United States attacked China would the Chinese fight. Wasn't that clear? Chinese were very busy with their internal affairs. Fighting beyond one's own borders was criminal. Why should the Chinese do so? The South Vietnamese could cope with their situation"* (emphasis in original). Mao interview with Snow, Jan. 9, 1965, Selected Works of Mao Tse-tung.

43. Before meeting with Johnson, Couve had told Bundy that he believed the Americans had already decided on escalation. See Bundy to Johnson, Feb. 19, 1965, *FRUS, 1984–1968*, 2: 330–31.

44. De Gaulle quoted in Yuko Torikata, "Reexamining de Gaulle's Peace Initiative on the Vietnam War," *Diplomatic History* 31, no. 5 (2007): 909–38.

45. De Gaulle press conference, Feb. 21, 1966, *Discours et Messages,* Vol. 5, 18.

46. Rusk quoted in Torikata, "Reexamining," 934.

47. Quoted in Lacouture, *Le Souverain,* 435.

Chapter 7

De Gaulle and the "Eternal China"

Lanxin Xiang

French emperor Napoleon Bonaparte purportedly made a statement that he probably never uttered and it has become a famous cliche: "When China awakes, the world will shake." Napoleon left no other comment on China. However, in a press conference on January 31, 1964, President Charles de Gaulle did pronounce a comprehensive view on China: "A fact of considerable significance is at work and is reshaping the world: China's very deep transformation puts her in a position to have a global leading role." He further stated that his decision to establish diplomatic relationships with communist China was motivated by his belief in the necessity of engaging an "eternal China" (*la Chine de toujours*), no matter its current political system and ideology.

From today's perspective, de Gaulle was farsighted. China's "peaceful rise" or "re-rise," was anticipated by him. He believed that the Chinese are a "people of patience, pride, industriousness," and "China is not a nation or a nation-state, but fundamentally is a civilization, a very unique and very deep civilization."[1] Today, the traditional elements of "eternal China" are at work once again and the Chinese renaissance has changed the world's distribution of power in a gradual and peaceful process. And so far, China's rise has not entailed abrupt discontinuity or violent disruption. The American neoconservative thesis of a Wilhelmian Germany analogy concerning China's rise can no longer hold water.

De Gaulle had never been to China but his China policy had made major contributions not only to the Sino-French relationship, but also to the ending and transformation of the entire Cold War system. Through diplomatic recognition of the People's Republic in 1964, de Gaulle succeeded in prying loose the rigid and militarized bipolar international system. Through his enormous charm and powerful logic in persuasion, he helped President Richard Nixon re-focus and clarify his thoughts on China policy, which directly led to the Sino-American rapprochement and the Detente and the rise of the Grand Strategic Triangle of Washington, Beijing, and Moscow.

COUNTERING THE AMERICANS:
DE GAULLE'S CHINA CARD DURING THE WAR

De Gaulle had used the China Card long before Henry Kissinger started considering it. Indeed, de Gaulle's decision to recognize Communist China in 1964 found its origins in an involved historical relationship between the two surviving wartime leaders of the anti-fascist alliance, General Chiang Kai-shek, who was president of China during the war, and General de Gaulle, the leader of Free France. In fact, although events beyond their control sometimes conspired to separate them, de Gaulle and Chiang Kai-shek had established a rather special relationship during the war against Japan. One aspect of this relationship was their shared feeling for being sidelined, or even snubbed by the Big Three of the allied leadership. Another aspect where de Gaulle and Chiang were in sympathy with each other concerned their unhappy relationship with the United States government in terms of the latter's habit of interfering in their internal affairs.

There was little doubt that the Roosevelt administration was vehemently against the return of European colonialism to the Asian-Pacific region. Such a stance undermined one of the primary objectives of the French war aims: to regain lost territories in Indo-China, "the pearl of the French colonial empire."

On August 15, 1945, the United States presented a diplomatic note to the Quai d'Orsay, announcing the U.S. decision to divide Indo-China into two zones for receiving the Japanese surrender, along the 16th parallel. Both the Americans and the British rejected de Gaulle's personal request for modifying this arrangement, but de Gaulle countered this decision by quickly appointing a "High Commissioner in charge of all affairs, air, land, and sea" for the purpose of re-establishing de facto French sovereignty in Indo-China.[2]

The French policy put Chiang Kai-shek in a difficult position. Unbeknownst to either Washington or London, the Chinese president and de Gaulle had already made a tacit agreement in 1944 in which Chiang promised not to interfere and obstruct France's return to the Tonkin. Chiang's motive was to gain French sympathy in his war efforts as well as domestic policy, as Roosevelt's military representative General Joseph Stilwell was making a lot trouble for him. Chiang's chief concern was how to eliminate the communist party after the war, while Stilwell insisted on giving top priority to fighting the Japanese and accused Chiang for evading serious democratic reforms of the Chinese internal system.[3]

Chiang had several secret meetings with de Gaulle's chief representative, General Zinovy Peshkov, to negotiate a deal with de Gaulle, promising to collaborate with him on the issue of how to defeat Ho Chi Minh's communist movement in Indo-China. Peshkov, a legendary figure in the French army, had family and personal connections with the Soviet Russia. An elder brother of Jakov Sverdlov, who was the young head of the state of the Soviet regime after the October Revolution, Peshkov went to Capri to follow his idol, the father of "socialist realist" writing, Maxim Gorky (he eventually took Gorky's family name, Peshkov) and served as his personal secretary before moving to French Canada and eventually ending up in Paris. De Gaulle always had a penchant for using colorful personalities to pursue secret missions (Edgar Faure and Andre Malraux were the other examples many years later). In his view, General Peshkov was perfect for the post in Chongqing, the wartime capital of China, representing Free France.

Peshkov knew very well that Chiang was in no mood for implementing the obligation announced at the Potsdam Conference, which included the Chinese taking over control of Vietnam and preventing the French from restoring colonial administration. But unfortunately, Chiang had no choice but to arrange for Chinese troops to enter Vietnam, after General McArthur issued General Order Number 1 on August 15, 1945. To outsiders and the Chinese population in general, such a move had the effect of enhancing Chinese international prestige. But Chiang's primary concern was how to defeat the Chinese Communists, whose military power and popularity had grown considerably during the war against Japan. The seemingly prestigious Indo-China mission was thus a red herring for him and an unnecessary distraction from his key objective of mobilizing troops for anti-communist operations.

In October 1944, T.V. Soong, the Chinese Foreign Minister wrote a letter to General Peshkov, asking for a comprehensive discussion of Sino-French relations. President Chiang used the occasion of the National Day celebrations on October 10, to receive Peshkov. In this secret meeting, Chiang emphasized that the "Spirit of the French people is closest to that of the Chinese, such cultural affinity is far beyond the level with the Anglo-Saxons." Chiang also expressed personal admiration for General de Gaulle. Chiang wanted to request General Stilwell's recall, and needed the support of de Gaulle. De Gaulle understood this message and he also needed to play the China card with the Americans and the British. Reacting quickly to Chiang's request for establishing diplomatic ties with Free France, de Gaulle hoped that the question of Indo-China would then be placed in the context of Sino-French diplomacy, free from the interference of the outsiders, the Anglo-Saxons and the Americans.

During T. V Soong's visit to Paris in September 1945, the Chinese Foreign Minister further declared that China "desires to see the French remain in China's neighbouring region." While Chiang made enormous efforts to keep his secret promise with de Gaulle and to facilitate the smooth return of France to Tonkin, events that took place on the spot went beyond his control. The Chinese commander in charge of receiving the Japanese surrender in Vietnam, General Lu Han, was a local warlord in Yunnan province. Never fully controlled by Chiang, Lu pursued a policy of preventing the French return. Worse still, Chiang's own personal representative, General Chen Xiuhe was not carrying out his instruction of pursuing only tepid opposition to the French return. General Chen was a first cousin of a famous Communist general Chen Yi (though Chiang only learned this in later years) and was secretly encouraging Ho Chi Minh to retard the French restoration of the colonial authority.[4]

By 1946, Chiang desperately needed to transfer his troops in Vietnam to engage the communists in Manchuria, and the French desired to restore colonial role as quickly as possible. Thus, de Gaulle and Chiang found common ground again. The result was a Sino-French agreement for Chinese military withdrawal, one that was not being undermined either by local Chinese warlords or Vietnamese communists who also had close links to the Chinese communist party.

In sum, the wartime story of the secret diplomacy between de Gaulle and Chiang was one of mutual success. Their respect for each other was genuine, and their friendship was to endure for decades. It was not surprising, when de Gaulle decided to establish diplomatic tie with Beijing, the person he sent to Taipei to console Chiang Kai-shek was none other than the retired General Zinovy Peshkov.

DIVERTING THE COLD WAR

In a January 1964 issue of *Time* magazine, the lead story started, "President Charles de Gaulle last week detonated a political bomb that scattered fallout from the Formosa Strait to Washington's Foggy Bottom. The blockbuster: France will 'soon' recognize Red China."

The United States got the word twice on the same day. In Paris, U.S. Ambassador Charles Bohlen was called to the Quai d'Orsay and was informed of France's intention. In Washington, "dapper French Ambassador Hervé Alphand gave the cold slap to Under Secretary of State Averill Harriman." The French government, said Alphand, considered it necessary "to fill the void" left by the Sino-Soviet dispute by accepting "the reality" of China.[5]

The French initiative caused an international sensation and generated intensive debate during the Cold War. This was the first time a major Western power had recognized Communist China since 1950, and de Gaulle re-entered the Asian stage like a diplomatic ice-breaker. The Cold War would never be the same again.

Many scholars accepted de Gaulle's claim that he was motivated by the "weight of evidence and reason." Fifteen years after the Chinese communist victory of the civil war, it became increasingly absurd to ignore the People's Republic of China's existence. But scholars disagree on other motives the French president may have had. Some stress his personal desire to demonstrate French *grandeur*; others for defining a middle path between the superpowers, a goal where China and France are natural allies. Still others argue that his sole motive was to embarrass the Americans.[6]

In fact, both de Gaulle and Mao were anti-Yalta world leaders. De Gaulle could not believe that an institutionalized bipolar Cold War structure would last very long. Mao had by that time lost faith in Moscow and become a leading rebel against Soviet dominance of the international communist camp. There were profound changes in de Gaulle's foreign policy around 1962. Two monumental events had convinced him that the Cold War needed a new context. The first was the Sino-Indian War and the second was the Cuban Missile Crisis. De Gaulle drew two lessons from the Cuban Missile Crisis. First he believed it showed that the two superpowers did not want a war, and second, that they would not risk a nuclear war for protecting their respective allies. In other words, the so-called nuclear umbrella was not reliable for French national security. As for the Sino-Indian war, he reached the conclusion that nationalism remained a dominant theme in international affairs, and it would eventually lead to a Sino-Soviet confrontation. As he told his cabinet ministers, "Both events are very important. They seem to have no connections, but they are related. The national element is becoming more and dominant. . . . It is the case for India against China, for China against the Russians."[7]

Thus de Gaulle and Mao joined hands for the purpose of providing the Cold War with a new direction, but such a move was considered by Washington as destructive of the U.S.-led containment strategy in Asia. It seems that the American side at that moment had little understanding of de Gaulle's motive and deep thought about China. And the U.S. government, especially President Lyndon Johnson and Secretary of State Dean Rusk, treated the

French decision to recognize China as another typical diplomatic prank by de Gaulle, part of his continuing personal revenge against the Americans dating from World War II.

Undersecretary of State Averill Harriman told French Ambassador Hervé Alphand that the French action would create doubt in Asia and would give a boost to Communist China. "French action would create great difficulty for people and government and President of United States It was clear decision had been taken with total disregard of important U.S. interests. France will be throwing away a great deal of good will and affection here in the United States only for the sake of demonstrating its independence of U.S. policy."

Harriman made it very clear that the French interference in Asian containment strategy was uncalled for and unwelcome. He stated that the United States had great responsibilities in the Far East, "although we welcomed France taking more responsibility in such places as Laos and Cambodia. However, the basic problem is containing Communist China and France can contribute very little as far as this basic problem is concerned" He made a further charge that, "Burden rests squarely on United States and France is strengthening our enemy. The Korean War has never been settled. Other areas of Asia are seething with Communist-supported conflicts. France has chosen the moment when our enemy is weak to help him."

Such language used by the Americans demonstrated once again a patronizing and condescending attitude toward France, all too familiar to de Gaulle during the Second World War. Also, de Gaulle would never accept the logic of the American accusation. The full recognition of Beijing's government was, above all, his personal decision. As one of France's greatest statesmen and a colossus of twentieth-century world politics, de Gaulle was present at the creation of the current international system and understood very well the defects of this system: the rigidity of the bipolar system could only maintain a very fragile balance.

He expected that U.S. policymakers would become highly agitated. Indeed, many in Washington viewed de Gaulle's action, undertaken without consulting his NATO allies, as simply a cheap way for France to demonstrate its independence in foreign affairs. According to *Time* magazine, Washington maintained that the French move was unwise because (1) it would not soften Red China's militancy; (2) it would upset the "very fragile balance" in the Far East and could have incalculable repercussions around the Chinese perimeter; (3) it would create an "acute" situation in the United Nations, since the additional votes of France, the French African states and, perhaps, Canada and Belgium could result in a seat for China's Communists.[8]

De Gaulle's spokesmen explained that the French president felt that the West should face up to the reality that "China exists," and take advantage of the Sino-Soviet split and the emergence of an independent China policy to open an avenue of contact with the vast human and geographic mass that China represented. But U.S. officials believed that de Gaulle had completely overlooked the fact that the United States was still keeping troops in South Korea, financing the Chinese Nationalist military effort on Taiwan, and was currently engaged in a war with Communism in South Vietnam.

The American government also encouraged the media to fan up anti-French sentiment. In the same issue, *Time* magazine put French Foreign Minister Maurice Couve de Murville on the cover, prompting many angry readers to react, including one who wrote a letter saying it was good to have him on the cover of a magazine with large circulation so that there would be thousands of opportunities to tear him up.

The Johnson administration was desperately seeking ways to repair the perceived damage, but in the Cold War context, an open fight with de Gaulle was deemed unwise in front of world public opinion. Besides, the French side stressed that no compromise had been made to Beijing concerning the status of the Franco-Taiwan relations. De Gaulle's personal representative for the Sino-French secret negotiation over the recognition issue was Edgar Faure, a former Gaullist Prime Minister. A key obstacle to the negotiation was the status of Taiwan. Faure was authorized by de Gaulle to tell Chinese Premier Zhou Enlai that General de Gaulle could not forget his wartime friendship with General Chiang Kai-shek, and France would not take the initiative to break diplomatic relations with Taiwan. Initially, Zhou Enlai was unwilling to yield an inch. There would be no "Two China policies" as suggested by France for maintaining diplomatic ties with Chiang.

But de Gaulle's role on the global stage was so significant in the eyes of Beijing that the Chinese side finally agreed to concede to the French demand, as Zhou told Faure that France and China had much in common. Both sides insisted on independent foreign policy and neither side had signed the Partial Nuclear Test Ban Treaty. France and China were in agreement that internal affairs should not be dominated by a couple of great powers and that a country's internal affairs were off limits to foreign interference. The final compromise concerning Taiwan was reflected by the Sino-French joint communiqué, perhaps the shortest ever about a significant move of establishing diplomatic relations between two important powers. It had only two sentences: "The government of the People's Republic of China and the government of the Republic of France have decided to establish diplomatic relations. The exchange of ambassadors will take place within three months." Taiwan was not mentioned at all.[9]

The Americans were angry. But it was considered unwise to confront France in a public fight. As President Johnson told Senator Richard Russell over the telephone, "About this de Gaulle thing, you just think we ought to play it as low key and just make a little protest for the record." Russell agreed. But the White House continued to seek for alternative strategies to sabotage de Gaulle's move. The best solution would be for Taiwan to play along with the American strategy.

In a conversation between the president and his Special Assistant for National Security Affairs, McGeorge Bundy, Bundy told the president, "The one chance that we can frustrate de Gaulle is to get Chiang to stand still for a week or so. If he would not break his relations with the French, which is what he's always done when people recognize Peking before, this would put the monkey right back on Peking's back, because they have maintained a position that they can't recognize anybody who also recognizes Formosa. What the French hope is that Chiang will break relations right away, and that is probably what he'll do. We want to advise him to stand still for a week. Is that all right with you?" Johnson agreed.

But the American strategy did not work, to the relief of de Gaulle. Chiang Kai-shek was unwilling to give up his self-claimed position as representative for all Chinese people in exchange for a diplomatic move that suited the American interest and offered dubious benefits to Taiwan. Any acceptance of a "Two China policy" would cause trouble for the Taiwan regime's legitimacy, as it would for Beijing's. After all, the Cairo and Potsdam declarations unambiguously called for the return of Taiwan to China. The U.S. government sent a CIA official, Ray Cline, to Taipei, and instructed him to see Chiang in person. But the Cline mission failed. He never had access to Chiang but had conversation with his son Chiang Ching-kuo instead. The Taiwan leader rejected the American proposal for delaying the act of breaking off diplomatic relations with Paris.[10]

DE GAULLE AND THE RISE OF THE
GRAND STRATEGIC TRIANGLE

To a large extent, détente was made in France. The concept itself was first proposed by de Gaulle. Both ideas for overcoming obstacles to ending the Vietnam War, and the opening of China by the United States originated with de Gaulle. Moreover, it was France who provided the physical setting for the top secret negotiations over a Vietnam peace agreement as well as a Sino-American rapprochement. The secret diplomacy was conducted on the U.S. side by Henry Kissinger.[11] Moreover, it was de Gaulle's personal influence on President Richard Nixon that started a new chapter of strategic rivalry between the United States and the Soviet Union, a chapter that led to the breakthrough in the relationship between Beijing and Washington and the eventual rise of a new Cold War system known as détente, which was characterized by a grand triangular diplomatic game played by the United States, China and the Soviet Union.

Richard Nixon often referred to the French president as Charles André Joseph Marie de Gaulle—a full name he thought would mean "grandeur, glory, greatness." De Gaulle was a peer of Roosevelt and Churchill, and Richard Nixon was overawed by such an outsized figure. The respect for each other extended to personality and politics. De Gaulle's book "The Edge of the Sword" was perhaps the most dog-eared and annotated in Nixon's private library. In its pages he found de Gaulle's claim that "Great men of action have without exception possessed to a very high degree the faculty of withdrawing into themselves." As early as the 1960 campaign, CBS reporter Nancy Dickerson noted that Nixon had "studied de Gaulle and was trying to emulate him."

Nixon revered de Gaulle and revelled in his company. Much of the affinity stemmed from the shared disdain for the fractious game of democratic politics, "Parliaments," de Gaulle wrote in another passage Nixon underlined, "can paralyze action but not initiate it." The psychological forces that drove Richard Nixon to the isolation of the Watergate scandal were no doubt fortified by the Gaullist presumptions.

Moreover, de Gaulle treated Nixon when he had been out of power as if he were a fellow head of state. At a dinner party in honor of Nixon at Elysee, de Gaulle lost no time urging American negotiations with China, introducing Nixon to the term détente, and toasting the former vice president's return to power "in an even higher capacity." After assuming the presidency, Nixon paid a visit to de Gaulle during a February 1969 trip. The French president once again urged Nixon to pursue a policy of détente with China as well as Russia.

De Gaulle's advice on China had a powerful logic. Dealing with Communist China as it had existed for two decades was the right approach. Notwithstanding the hardships caused by Mao's bad policy of the Great Leap Forward, China had bounced back in the 1960s, its economy by no means destroyed by internal disruption during the Cultural Revolution. Moreover, Mao was in firm control of the country and his relationship with the Soviet Union had turned from tepid friendship into outright hostility. As de Gaulle explained in 1964, "there is no doubt some ideological affiliation between Moscow and Beijing, but behind the mask, increasingly we see the inevitable differences in policies between the two."

The most important factor that had inspired Nixon was the virtual political monopoly of the Republican Party to dictate any changes in America's China policy. The Democratic Party was so demoralized by its failure in China during the late 1940s and early 1950s that China policy had long become taboo. Indeed, it was Joe McCarthy and Richard Nixon himself, a young congressman from southern California, who had destroyed the credibility and careers of those who handled China under the Roosevelt and Truman Administrations.

Since the Korean War, no Democratic administration or members of Congress dared to touch the issue of China policy, knowing that the Republicans would destroy anyone who suggested drastic changes of the American stance of a tough containment strategy against Beijing. Thus Nixon realized that he would be in a unique historic position to make changes without carrying the "pro-communist" stigma. As for the need for secret diplomacy regarding China, Nixon and de Gaulle could not agree with each other more. De Gaulle's motto was "Parliaments can paralyze action but not initiate it." Nixon always had always been paranoid about democratic decision-making procedures.

Moreover, Nixon was fascinated by de Gaulle's penchant for personal diplomacy and the personalities chosen for carrying out this type of action. It is not surprising that Henry Kissinger fitted the needs for secret diplomacy very well, as the latter was of the same mind concerning formal political processes. Edgar Faure's secret diplomacy with Beijing started as early as 1958 and de Gaulle was keenly interested in every detail of Faure's visits to China in his private capacity. Faure's conversations with Mao covered a variety of subjects, such as culture, history, and poetry. De Gaulle understood these conversations through his exceptionally acute historical and cultural sense.

His special envoy to China after the establishment of diplomatic ties was Andre Malraux, through whom de Gaulle was able to grasp the very sophisticated political symbolism between France and China. Although Malraux's imagination could go a bit too far, as he was often accused of fictionalizing politics and politicizing fiction, he did provide de Gaulle with a cultural lens for understanding the continuity between the long Chinese history and the communist revolution, a continuity he called the "Eternal China," and grasping the essence of China's internal affairs.[12] Malraux also played an important role in educating the Nixon administration about China both when de Gaulle was in office and after de Gaulle's death, paying two visits to the White House in 1972, and conferring with President Nixon prior to his visit to China.

THE GAULLIST SPIRIT IS ALIVE

De Gaulle's last wish was to visit Mao in China. Since this historic meeting between two giants of the twentieth century did not ultimately take place, one could entertain endless speculation about what such a meeting might have included. One near certainty is that they would have had a profound exchange about history. Claude Chayet was the first French diplomat to arrive in Beijing for making arrangements to reopen the French embassy. He was summoned by de Gaulle in February 1964 for instructions. One question Chayet raised with the President was whether he should reclaim the old French embassy building. He explained that it was located in the old legation quarter, a source of very bad memory for the Chinese due to the Boxer War. Chayet suggested that the French should not carry this "burden of history." De Gaulle said to him firmly, "Which country doe not have the burden of history? You just go ahead to reclaim this embassy."[13]

According to de Gaulle's son Philippe, de Gaulle truly wished to visit China and shortly before his death, former Foreign Minister Couve de Murville went to Beijing in September 1970 to arrange the General's visit. Couve met Mao in Beijing and the Chinese leader expressed his great admiration for a "symbol of an independent country." In the meantime, the Belgian-Chinese writer Han Su-Yin who was a personal friend of Zhou Enlai went to see Jacques Rueff, conveying Zhou's message that the Chinese government would welcome a visit by the General at any time of his convenience. Rueff wrote to the General and also asked Couve to return to Beijing in November. But it was too late. De Gaulle passed away on November 10, 1970.[14] Two months before his death, de Gaulle told his niece, Marie-Thérèse de Corbie, who was posted in the Beijing embassy as cultural counsellor, that he would "rever" the opportunity to have a dialogue with Chairman Mao.[15]

Both the Chinese and the French sides have since kept General de Gaulle's spirit alive. The two governments frequently invoke the image of de Gaulle when the two countries are in dispute, such as over the French submarine sales to Taiwan in the 1980s or the current row over Tibet. In good times, de Gaulle's image is equally important. When the Chinese President Hu Jintao visited Paris in January 2004, he made a point to visit the Charles de Gaulle Foundation. When Sarkozy tried to overcome the Sino-French stalemate over Dalai Lama and the Olympics, he sent a biography of de Gaulle as a present to the Chinese leader. Despite recent diplomatic difficulties between Beijing and Paris, the two countries continued to share many common interests, especially during the current economic crisis.

When President Sarkozy went to Washington in November 2007, he spoke to Congress and told the United States to stop dumping dollars on the rest of the world, "The dollar cannot remain solely the problem of others," He was referring to the bad joke made by John Connally, Treasury Secretary to Richard Nixon in the early 1970s. Connally told the world infamously that the dollar was America's currency "but your problem." It weighs heavily with history. "What the United States owes to foreign countries it pays—at least in part—with dollars that it can simply issue if it chooses to," complained the French president Charles de Gaulle in a landmark press conference of February, 1965.

The Chinese did not understand de Gaulle's logic then, but they do now. Only recently, the Chinese state was absent-mindedly entangled by a huge pool of dollar assets in the form of the U.S. treasuries, and found these assets in danger of depreciation and outright loss. The Chinese began to appreciate de Gaulle's view: "This unilateral facility contributes to the gradual disappearance of the idea that the dollar is an impartial and international trade medium, whereas it is in fact a credit instrument reserved for one state only." Unlike the Chinese leaders, however, de Gaulle still had the chance to exchange his dollars for a real asset—gold bullion—at the window of the Federal Reserve.

The conditions for genuinely mutual understanding between France and China are more conducive than in the past. China, for its part, is ready. In an interview with the French newspaper *Le Figaro,* Prime Minister Wen Jiabao made a very important remark when quoting Gu Hongming, a colourful nineteenth century Confucian scholar who was also educated in the west. Premier Wen declared that "in this world, perhaps only the French could best understand China and Chinese civilization, because the French possess the same almost unique spiritual quality as the Chinese—subtlety." Significantly, this statement can also be said to sum up China's attitude towards the European Union as a whole.[16]

Looked at in terms of China's foreign policy logic, Mr. Wen's "spiritual subtlety" seems to have three dimensions. First, China rejects the traditional eurocentric view of human history, and in this has found intellectual allies in Europe. The eurocentric view assumes the inherent superiority of Greco-Roman civilization and sustains the myth that Europe's achievements derived from its cultural originality, technical innovation, and free human spirit. Europe is thus chosen to be the only "unbound Prometheus" in human history, so the rest of the world, including China, has perforce been backward, despotic, and barbaric.

Second, China hopes to work with the EU in dismantling the last bastion of the power theory of international relations that is so deeply embedded in the current system. The EU is the first multinational political entity that has officially moved beyond the age-old logic of balance of power and hegemony. Its "spiritual subtlety" also helps the EU move beyond a "good and evil" view of the world. This fits very well with the Chinese call for the "democratization of international relations" (*Guoji Guanxi Mingzhuhua*). Now that international rules and institutions are becoming crucial in China's foreign policy decision-making, multipolarity, and multilateralism have begun to unify the entire Eurasian continent and are a result of the intense institution-building activity in the region that has been inspired by the EU's success.

Third, the idea that the Sino-French relationship can only flourish at the expenses of transatlantic relations is perceived by Beijing to be a "Cold War mentality" (*Lengzhan Siwei*) that is as absurd as the idea that China will remain under the tutelage of the western-dictated globalization. As far as China is concerned, the political and ideological west is disappearing, and harmony among civilizations has instead been placed on the global agenda. The lessons of history continue to have their impact on the two major players on the global stage. As in the days of General de Gaulle, the cornerstone of the Sino-French relationship remains independent foreign and security policy and the common fight against any residual thinking of a unipolar world.

NOTES

1. www.charles-de-gaulle.org/pages/l-homme/dossiers-thematiques/de-gaulle-et-le-monde/de-gaulle-et-la-reconnaissance-de-la-chine/documents/31-janvier-1964--conference-de-presse-du-general-de-gaulle.php.

2. Charles de Gaulle, *Lettres et carnets* (Paris: Plon, 1984), p. 58.

3. For details about the Stilwell-Chiang affair, see Barbara Tuchman, *Stilwell and the American Experience in China, 1911–45* (Grove Press, 2001).

4. Lin Hua, *Chiang Kai-shek, De Gaulle contre Ho Chi Minh, Vietnam, 1945–1946*, p. 60 to 65 (Paris: L'Harmattan, 1994).

5. "France: The Cold Slap," *Time* magazine, Friday, Jan. 24, 1964.

6. "France: The Cold Slap," *Time* magazine, Friday, Jan. 24, 1964

7. Garret Martin, "Playing the China Card? Revisiting France's Recognition of Communist China, 1963–1964", *Journal of Cold War Studies*, Vol. 10, No. 1 Winter 2008, p. 59.

8. "France: The Cold Slap," *Time* magazine, Friday, Jan. 24, 1964.

9. For the details on the Chinese side, see Ambassador Cai Fangbai (former Ambassador to France and a participant in the secret negotiations), "The Secret Negotiations between China and France over mutual diplomatic recognition," and interview, http://webcast.china.com.cn/webcast/created/2868/44_1_0101_desc.htm.

10. For intense diplomacy over this issue, see, Second Taiwan Strait Crisis Quemoy and Matsu Islands—23 August 1958–01 January 1959. FOREIGN RELATIONS OF THE UNITED STATES 1964–1968 Volume XXX, China.

11. See Henry Kissinger, *The White House Years* (Boston: Little Brown, 1979).

12. For de Gaulle's extraordinary relationship with Malraux, see Christine Clerc, *De Gaulle-Malraux: Une histoire d'amour*, NIL , 2008.

13. Interview with Claude Chayet, the Charles de Gaulle Foundation, http://www.charles-de-gaulle.org/pages/l-homme/dossiers-thematiques/de-gaulle-et-le-monde/

de-gaulle-et-la-reconnaissance-de-la-chine/temoignages/claude-chayet--premier-representant-de-la-france-a-pekin-en-1964.php.

14. Philippe de Gaulle, Memoires accessoires (Paris: Plon, 1997), Chapter 7.

15. *De Gaulle et la Reconnaissance de la Chine*. http://www.charles-de-gaulle. org/pages/l-homme/dossiers-thematiques/de-gaulle-et-le-monde/de-gaulle-et-la-reconnaissance-de-la-chine.php?searchresult=1&sstring=chine.

16. *Le Figaro*, December 2, 2005.

Chapter 8

De Gaulle and the Middle East Conflict

Timo Behr

On November 27, 1967, President Charles de Gaulle held a landmark press conference, addressing the outcome of the Arab-Israeli Six Day War. In his statement, de Gaulle condemned Israeli aggression in no uncertain terms, warning that a lasting occupation of the conquered territories would fuel Arab resistance and stand in the way of a permanent settlement. Denouncing the "scandalous fate of the refugees in Jordan" and demanding international status to be conferred on Jerusalem, de Gaulle remarked: "Israel attacked, and reached its objectives in six days of fighting. Now it organizes itself on conquered territories, the occupation of which cannot go without oppression, repression, expulsions, while at the same time a resistance grows, which it regards as terrorism."[1]

At the time, de Gaulle's statement evoked much controversy. His contentious description of Jews as "an elite people, sure of themselves and domineering" that would "once assembled again on the land of their ancient greatness, turn into a burning and conquering ambition" drew the ire of no less a political and moral authority than Raymond Aron.[2] His comprehensive repositioning of French policies in the Middle East following the crisis and his rupture of the Fourth Republic's 'tacit alliance' with Israel were opposed by a majority of the French public, which remained deeply sympathetic to the Zionist cause. And French officials repeatedly attempted to challenge and circumvent the tightening arms embargo de Gaulle sought to enforce on France's erstwhile ally.[3]

From today's perspective, however, de Gaulle's words appear to have had a near prophetic quality; foretelling the decades of uninterrupted bloodshed that followed while correctly identifying what would be the necessary ingredients for a sustainable solution to the enduring conflict. His Middle Eastern realignment also left a profound mark on European diplomacy. It cemented French claims to be a Middle Eastern power and allowed de Gaulle's successors to work assiduously against superpower subjugation of the region. More importantly, de Gaulle's policies planted the seeds of an independent European policy in the Middle East that would only come to germinate much later.

Although time seems to have proven de Gaulle right once again, the motives for his Middle Eastern *volte-face* remain as disputed today as they were back then.[4] The literature on de Gaulle's foreign policy has offered a variety of explanations for his policy-shift. Some have argued that his decision was primarily a strategic move to earn the goodwill of the Arabs,[5] while others have seen in it an attempt to placate the Soviet Union in order to complete a budding Franco-Soviet entente.[6] More benign interpretations either tend to emphasize de Gaulle's disquiet with the Cold War balance[7]—citing his concerns over a new global war—or his apprehensions about the outcome of the Six Day War on the balance and stability of the Middle Eastern regional system.[8]

But are any of these explanations adequate to account for de Gaulle's behavior during the Six Day War? Could his decision to break France's tacit alliance with Israel really have been a well-prepared strategic realignment, rather than an emotional reaction to Israeli intransigence? Did his actions constitute a 'normalization' of French policies in the Middle East following a hiatus during the Fourth Republic, or did he 'reinvent' and reorient France's role in the region?[9] How did de Gaulle arrive at his position? And what are the lessons that can be drawn from this episode that are still of relevance today? Any attempt at explanation begins with the Fourth Republic's record in the region.

THE FOURTH REPUBLIC AND
THE TACIT ALLIANCE WITH ISRAEL

To most historians the Fourth Republic represents a brief interlude to France's traditionally close ties with the Arab world; a historical parenthesis to a long-running relationship that is deeply rooted in French history, geography and strategic interests.[10] To these historians, the break with tradition was a result of France's post-war weakness, which left France militarily and mentally ill-prepared to either crush the growing tide of Arab nationalism or pursue a peaceful settlement. At home, the Republic's weak institutions undermined central control, thereby permitting "Israel to capitalize on the reservoir of pro-Jewish sentiment that existed in France."[11] A close alliance with Israel was thus the inevitable result of French weakness. When de Gaulle returned France to a position of strength, French diplomacy reverted to its long-term trajectory.

France's troubles in the Middle East began with the end of the French mandate in Syria and Lebanon in 1946. The end of the mandate not only weakened the Fourth Republic's influence in the region, but also foreshadowed the future battle lines. Forced to abandon its centuries-old position in the Levant as a result of British pressure, de Gaulle fumed about the treachery of 'perfidious Albion' and pledged revenge.[12] According to David Styan, it was during the period of Anglo-French rivalry in the Levant that de Gaulle "became convinced that Britain's principal aim was to usurp French influence in the Middle East, hardening his conviction that all Arab nationalist agitation simply reflected British manipulation."[13] While that might overstate the point, French officials thereafter remained suspicious of Anglo-Saxon intentions in the region.

The brief postwar honeymoon between the western allies in the Middle East was therefore unsurprisingly short-lived. In a nod to historical French interests, the Anglo-Saxon duo invited France to join the Tripartite Declaration of 1950 which sought to limit the flow of arms to the Middle East in order to back up the tenuous status quo that followed Israel's creation.[14] The Declaration did indeed succeed in limiting the flow of arms to the region. However, the intrusion of the Cold War into Middle Eastern politics encouraged the United States and the UK to pursue the establishment of a collective security system for the region. The 1955 Baghdad Pact created a northern tier alliance between Iran, Iraq, Turkey and Pakistan that was led by Britain and sanctioned by the United States. This new alliance undermined the Tripartite Agreement and left France dangerously isolated.[15]

French officials vehemently objected to the establishment of the Baghdad Pact which they regarded as a thinly-veiled attempt to consolidate British influence in the Eastern Mediterranean. France's principal fear was that by turning Iraq into the most highly armed power in the region, the Baghdad Pact would favor the creation of a Greater Syria under Hashemite control.[16] Encouraged by Britain, Iraq's Hashemite rulers had long laid claim to French dominated Syria. With the conclusion of the Baghdad Pact, they would now have the means to substantiate that claim. Moreover, French diplomats correctly lamented that the Baghdad Pact would invariably split the region between a revolutionary and a reactionary camp and invite rather than forestall Soviet intervention. French fears were confirmed when President Gamal Abdel Nasser of Egypt signed an arms deal with Czechoslovakia in 1955 that kicked off a new Middle East arms race.

At the same time that the Fourth Republic found itself sidelined by the Anglo-Saxon duo in the Levant, its North African possessions faced a growing threat from nationalist liberation movements. Protests and resistance spread throughout Tunisia and Morocco in the early 1950s, leading to their independence by 1956. But when violence spilled over into Algeria in 1954, French officials decided to make a stand. As France's largest North African possession, with a considerable *pied-noir* population, Algeria represented more than just a strategic asset on its Mediterranean doorstep. To French diplomats and officers railing from their defeat at Dien Bien Phu, Algeria symbolized the last chance to conserve French international power; the last remnant of *la plus grand France.*[17]

As the Algerian drama unfolded and violence slowly spiraled out of control, France found itself increasingly isolated and exposed to international criticism.[18] It was at this vital juncture that the Fourth Republic's tacit alliance with Israel was forged. A shared enmity towards Nasser's Egypt and a deep mistrust of Anglo-Saxon stratagems for the region, proved a strong short-term adhesive. The fragmented nature of the Fourth Republic and the strong pro-Israeli leanings of a number of key French officials—amongst them luminaries such as Maurice Bourgès-Maunoury, Christian Pineau, Pierre Koenig and Jacques Soustelle—served to sideline the traditionally pro-Arab Quai d'Orsay and to favor the establishment of an alliance based on unorthodox diplomacy.

Relations with Israel began to warm in 1953 when France agreed to ignore its arms limitation commitments under the Tripartite Declaration in order to supply the Israeli Defense Forces (IDF) with AMX-13 tanks and small weapons, and to engage in some limited cooperation in the nuclear field.[19] More arms contracts soon followed, solicited by Shimon Peres, director at the Israeli defense ministry, and Pierre Gilbert, France's ambassador to Israel. In 1955, the purchase of Mystère IV fighter bombers by Israel, against explicit British warnings that they threatened to unhinge the military balance of the region, triggered widespread speculations about a looming Franco-Israeli military alliance.[20] French obsessions about Nasser's meddling in Algeria, at times skillfully manipulated by Israeli intelligence, soon provided the rationale for joint military planning leading to the fateful Suez intervention of 1956.[21]

Humiliated by the United States, deserted by the UK and isolated by the Arabs, France and Israel were pressed ever closer together following the Suez debacle. Relations continued to be especially close throughout the term of the Socialist government under Guy Mollet, which was sympathetic to Israel's continued occupation of Gaza.[22] Bilateral cooperation on nuclear technology intensified, centered on Israel's Dimona reactor, and weapons sales continued apace.[23] In particular, large-scale sales of French Mystère and Mirage aircraft allowed Israel to attain the aerial dominance that was to be the decisive factor for its crushing victory in 1967. While bilateral relations became more distant following the fall of the Mollet government in 1957, close ties between the two defense establishments ensured that defense and nuclear cooperation survived the death throes of the Fourth Republic.

THE FIFTH REPUBLIC AND
THE SEARCH FOR MIDDLE EASTERN BALANCE

Upon his return to power in 1958, de Gaulle's major goal was to restore France to her place amongst the Great Powers. Reclaiming France's former position in the Middle East was naturally part of the objective. De Gaulle acknowledged as much in his *Memoirs:* "In the Middle East our affairs are at an all-time low. The Algerian crisis and the Suez incident have closed off our access to the Arab states. . . . . Naturally, I intend to reestablish our position in this region of the world, where France has always been active."[24]

To de Gaulle, the extent to which France's position in the region had deteriorated was further underlined by the 1958 Middle East crisis. The establishment of the United Arab Republic (UAR) that year rattled some of the pro-Western governments of the region. As rising tensions threatened to sweep away the Jordanian and Lebanese governments, Eisenhower and Macmillan coordinated an intervention to rescue their clients.[25] This joint Anglo-Saxon intervention in a traditional French sphere, without prior consultation, demonstrated the full extent of French weakness and left de Gaulle fuming.

In his attempt to change French fortunes in the region, de Gaulle sought to break France's isolation amongst the Arab countries. To this end, he pursued a normalization of relations with Israel and a greater balance in his approach towards the region. While the ongoing war in Algeria prevented the re-launching of full diplomatic ties with the Arab states until 1962, de Gaulle acted swiftly to put relations with Israel on a more official footing.

As a first step, de Gaulle announced his plans to sever nuclear cooperation with all third countries during the first meeting of the National Security Council on 17 June 1958.[26] In his memoirs de Gaulle later recalled ending the "improper military collaboration established between Tel Aviv and Paris after the Suez Expedition, which permanently placed Israelis at all levels of French services."[27] Maurice Couve de Murville simultaneously was tasked to restore the control of the Quai d'Orsay over French diplomacy. However, resistance to these measures amongst French officials meant that Franco-Israeli nuclear cooperation continued for some time in a clandestine fashion.[28]

But while de Gaulle was eager to end the unnatural relations that had allowed Israeli officials direct access to the highest level of French military and nuclear programs, he had no interest in terminating the Franco-Israeli partnership. De Gaulle welcomed Ben Gurion for a state visit to Paris on 14 June 1960, during which he expressed his admiration for the "marvelous resurrection, renaissance, pride, and prosperity of Israel" and promised to continue French support.[29] Similarly, during a meeting with Prime Minister Eshkol in 1964, de Gaulle described Israel as an "ally and friend," confirming his commitment to the security of Israel "even if that meant destroying Cairo."[30] Close cooperation between the defense and intelligence establishments of both countries continued for several years, while France remained Israel's major arms supplier right until the eve of the Six Day War. Nevertheless, as Israeli historian Gadi Heimann noted, the relationship increasingly lost its former ideological-emotional dimension, turning instead into a classical patron-client relationship with France in the driver's seat.[31]

While maintaining close ties with Israel, de Gaulle was eager to complement these by reviving diplomatic relations with the Arab world. Despite Couve's best efforts to negotiate a settlement of financial disputes with Egypt, however, relations remained stymied until the signing of the Evian Accords in 1962.[32] The following years saw a rapid improvement in Franco-Arab ties. The reestablishment of formal diplomatic relations in 1962–1963 was followed by a flurry of visits from Arab dignitaries, culminating in a trip of Egypt's Field Marshall 'Abd al-Hakim Amer to Paris in 1965. In 1963, the sale of Mirage aircraft and Alouette helicopters to Jordan also signaled the beginning of a more active French armaments policy.[33] Finally, the signing of a large contract for the delivery of Algerian oil in 1965 allowed France for the first time to break into the Anglo-Saxon oil monopoly.

The revival of relations with the Arab world was also a vital component to de Gaulle's overall geopolitical strategy. Following the failure of the French plans for Europe in 1962, de Gaulle increasingly turned to the Third World.[34] His intention was to tap the dynamism and potential of Third World nationalism to check the growing global dominance of the superpowers. In the Middle East that necessitated closer ties with Algeria and Egypt as two of the champions of the non-aligned movement.[35] Moreover, de Gaulle noted with concern the growing activism of U.S. policies in the region, which he feared would automatically "harden Cold War rivalry, polarize the policies in the Middle East, upset the intra-Arab regional arms balance, and add to the threat of local war and even of a global conflict."[36] To forestall any further superpower intrusion into regional politics, he hoped to position France as a third force and mediator between the two sides.

Throughout, de Gaulle did not see any contradictions between being Israel's major arms supplier and pursuing closer ties with the Arab world. Instead, he attempted to use his influence with Israel to boost France's value with the Arabs and the superpowers and substantiate French claims to being a regional mediator. Arab countries did indeed increasingly seek French mediation in their conflicts with Israel—whether concerning Israeli-Syrian border tensions in 1962 or the Israeli-Lebanese dispute over the waters of the Hatzbani River.[37] However, this meant that France's credibility as a regional player strongly depended on its ability to reign in its Israeli client. Given the context of greater superpower confrontation as well as the deepening of Arab-Israeli hostilities after 1962, this claim became ever more tenuous, preparing for the eventual fraying of Franco-Israeli ties.

Border incidents between Israel and its Arab neighbors began to multiply after 1962. Most followed a similar pattern. Small-scale incursions of Arab *fedayeen* were regularly followed by larger and often disproportionate reprisals by Israeli forces. One such reprisal in 1965 led to the near destruction of the Lebanese village of Hula by an Israeli unit, leaving some 50 dead and scores wounded.[38] Repeated attempts by France to restrain its Israeli client went unheeded and only served the purpose of further undermining its credibility with the Arabs while upsetting its relations with Israel. French criticism of Israel grew more intense following the Hula reprisal, with de Gaulle becoming increasingly frustrated about Israeli intransigence.

Simultaneously, Israel's reliance on France as its major ally and weapons supplier began to weaken. By the time of Ben Gurion's unsuccessful call for a formalization of the alliance following the establishment of the UAR in 1963, the high point of Franco-Israeli relations had passed. With the election of the more pro-American Levi Eshkol as Israel's new Prime Minister the same year, Israel increasingly looked for support across the Atlantic. A first arms deal with the United States in 1963 was followed by large-scale purchases of Skyhawk bombers and Patton tanks in 1965, ending France's monopoly as weapons supplier.[39] Although some of these purchases were dictated by Israel's changing weapon needs, a further weakening of French influence was the inevitable outcome. Bilateral relations also frayed in other areas, with annual meetings of the general staffs of both countries being suspended in 1961 and intelligence cooperation ending in 1966. After years in which de Gaulle favored a balanced an evenhanded approach in the region, the scene was now set for the inevitable confrontation that would end the last remnants of the tacit alliance.

DE GAULLE, THE SIX DAY WAR AND THE "POLITIQUE ARABE"

The crisis arrived when Egyptian troops streamed into the demilitarized Sinai on May 14 and 15, 1967, following inaccurate Soviet reports that Israel was assembling its forces for a large-scale assault on Syria. Israel responded by calling up reserves and threatening war. De Gaulle, convinced that the Israeli side was exaggerating the threat in order to provoke a showdown with Nasser, regarded the looming confrontation as a serious challenge to French interests. Any confrontation would inevitably lead to an escalation of tension between the superpowers in the region. At best, this would diminish French influence in the Middle East. At worst, this could provoke a new global war. An Israeli attack would also force France to take sides and show up its limitations as a mediator in regional affairs. Worse yet, France's failure in the Middle East would weaken its claim to be a global power.

To prevent a potentially damaging confrontation, de Gaulle attempted to mediate between the conflict parties. Initially, France seemed well positioned. While the United States and the UK asked de Gaulle to use his influence to restrain Nasser, the Soviets called upon him to moderate Israel. The strategy of maintaining balanced but close relations with both sides seemed to pay off. However, when Nasser decided to close the Straits of Tiran on May 22, war drew closer. De Gaulle reacted by calling for a conference of the four powers to resolve the crisis and by urging Israel to refrain from firing the first shot.

In a meeting with Israeli Foreign Minister Abba Eban on May 24, de Gaulle rejected Israel's reading of the situation and made clear that France would not aid in a forceful opening of the Straits.[40] During the meeting, de Gaulle admonished Eban, "Don't make war. You will be considered the aggressor by the world and me. You will cause the Soviet Union to penetrate more deeply into the Middle East, and Israel will suffer the consequences. You will create a Palestinian nationalism, and you will never get rid of it."[41] Eban retorted that Egypt had fired the first shot when it closed the Straits and that Israel would refuse to make any concession as part of a four power agreement. According to Sylvia Crosbie, the meeting "ended once and for all any illusion that Israel's favored relationship with France had survived."[42]

Confronted with Israeli reticence, De Gaulle decided to increase the pressure. On June 2, he declared an embargo on the shipment of arms to the Middle East and called for a four-power agreement to settle the issue of the Straits, as well as the question of refugees and Israel's borders. On both issues, his hand had been forced. De Gaulle's decision to enforce an arms embargo followed prior press reports about large-scale arms purchases by Israel which appeared to contradict French claims of neutrality and even-handedness. On the four-power agreement, de Gaulle had little choice but to concede to Kosygin's demand that any agreements would have to include Israeli concessions.[43]

In a meeting with Israel's ambassador Walter Eytan the following day, de Gaulle assured him that the embargo would be lifted once the crisis had passed and warned him against the serious long-term consequences of war. In his report of the meeting Eytan wrote: "He [de Gaulle] believes that war will bring a catastrophe upon us even if we win. We will suffer heavy losses. The Arabs will bomb our cities, and in the end instead of solving the problem we will only magnify hatred."[44] When Israel initiated hostilities on June 5, the limits of French influence over Israel became apparent. De Gaulle admitted as much, stating: "Israel has nothing to ask from us, and we have nothing to offer it."[45]

Following the war, de Gaulle once again attempted to obtain a four-power agreement to settle the outcome of the conflict. But heightened tension resulting from the situation in Vietnam prevented any agreement amongst the superpowers. Although de Gaulle initially seemed inclined to grant Israel some territorial concessions following the war, he subsequently voted in favor of a Yugoslav resolution at the UN that called for a full Israeli withdrawal to the armistice lines of 1949.[46] His denunciation of Israeli as the sole aggressor following the end of hostilities and his much-noted press conference condemning Israel's occupation of the conquered territory ended de Gaulle's attempt to play best friend to both sides and realigned France more firmly with the Arab states.

In the years that followed, relations between France and Israel further deteriorated. In 1968, an Israeli raid on Beirut airport resulted in a further tightening of the French arms embargo that until then had only been lightly implemented. While this meant that Israel increasingly turned to the United States as its new weapons supplier of choice, large weapon orders from the Arab states more than compensated France for the loss of its oldest customer.[47] In consequence, greater concessions for French energy companies in the Arab states, and especially Iraq, followed.[48] Under de Gaulle's successors these commercial aspects of the relationship would come to dominate the Fifth Republic's budding *politique arabe*. On his visit to Paris in 1968, President Arif of Iraq summed up the impact of the crisis, declaring that in the Middle East, France "is in the process of winning hearts, just as the English sun is setting and the tyranny of the Americans is coming to a close."[49]

Considering the evolution of de Gaulle's policies towards the Middle East conflict, it appears that his decision to break France's tacit alliance with Israel was neither based on a short-sighted emotional reaction nor a long-term strategy of aligning himself with the Arab countries. Rather, de Gaulle seems to have attempted, albeit unsuccessfully, to maintain close ties with both conflict parties. The Six Day War showed the limits of this balanced approach by demonstrating de Gaulle's failure to influence the decisions of his Israeli client. His subsequent choice to opt for closer ties with the Arab states was the consequence of his reading of the regional and global geopolitical context.

In the Middle East, de Gaulle considered that Israel had overreached itself and had become a major cause of regional instability. In a letter to Ben Gurion, de Gaulle wrote:

But I remain convinced that by ignoring the warning given in good time to your government by the French government, by taking possession of Jerusalem and of many Jordanian, Egyptian and Syrian territories by force of arms, by exercising repression and expulsion there . . . by affirming to the world that a settlement of the conflict could only be achieved on the basis of the conquests made and not on the condition that they be evacuated, Israel is overstepping the bounds of necessary moderation.[50]

In the global context, de Gaulle's decision was motivated by his desire to disassociate French policies from the United States and place France at the head of a third force in world politics that would serve French independence and grandeur. While some have tried to explain de Gaulle's eagerness to placate the Soviet Union during the crisis as signaling an overriding desire to bring about a potential Franco-Soviet entente, this interpretation seems unlikely given his goal of staying clear of superpower tutelage.[51] More likely, de Gaulle's actions were, as always, dictated by what he regarded to be France's own national interests. As Jean Lacouture correctly remarked, "If de Gaulle had wanted to barter the affection of the Arabs against the admiration of the Israelis, he certainly succeeded. But we know that was not—and never was—his purpose. A friend neither of the Arabs, nor of Israel, but only of France."[52]

De Gaulle's decision has had a profound impact on French and international politics in the region. His realignment of French policies in the Middle East marked the beginning of France's *politique arabe,* which soon became a trademark of the Fifth Republic's international politics. His outspoken denouncement of Israeli policies allowed his successors to pose as champions of the Arab and Palestinian cause and anticipated a swing of French public opinion concerning the conflict. Finally, by opting for an activist and autonomous French policy in the region, de Gaulle planted the seed for an independent European policy on the Middle East conflict developed by his successors.

If there are any lessons to be learnt from this episode for the current situation in the region, it is the difficulty of adopting a balanced approach. Like the United States today, de Gaulle attempted to play best friend to both sides in the conflict. This allowed France to claim a special role in the region. But this claim was only credible for as long as France managed to influence both sides and prevent a major conflict. When matters came to a head in 1967, de Gaulle courageously played his last ace—the arms embargo—in order to restrain Israel and preserve France's standing in the region. When this failed, de Gaulle accepted the costs of confronting France's pro-Israeli public and political elite in order to preserve what he regarded as France's geopolitical interests. His decision allowed his successors to maintain a modicum of influence in this strategically important region. Whether the current U.S. administration is going to be willing to make a similarly courageous decision—in case its attempts at a more balanced approach should fail—remains to be seen.

BIBLIOGRAPHY

Ageron, Charles-Robert (1989). *"L'Algérie, dernière chance de la puissance française: Étude d'une mythe politique* (1954–1962)," *Relations Internationales*, 57, pp. 113–39.

Aron, Raymond (1968). *De Gaulle, Israël et les Juifs.* Paris: Plon.

Aruri, Nasser H. & Natalie Hevener (1969). "France and the Middle East, 1967–1968," *Middle East Journal*, 23:4, 484–502.

Bar-Zohar, Michel (1986). *Histoire secrète de la guerre d'Israël.* Paris: Fayard.

Cohen, Avner (1998). *Israel and the Bomb.* New York: Columbia University Press.

Crosbie, Sylvia Kowitt (1974). *A Tacit Alliance: France and Israel from Suez to the Six Day War.* Princeton, N. J.: Princeton University Press.

De Gaulle, Charles (1970). *Mémoires d'Espoir.* Paris: Plon.

De la Gorce, Paul-Marie (1999). *De Gaulle.* Paris: Perrin.

Heiman, Gadi (2010). "Diverging Goals: the French and Israeli Pursuit of the Bomb, 1958–1962," *Israel Studies*, 15:2, pp. 104–26.

Heimann, Gadi (2010a). "In Search of a Route to World Power: General de Gaulle, the Soviet Union, and Israel in the Middle Eastern Crisis of 1967," *The International History Review* 32:1, pp. 69–88.

Heimann, Gadi (2010b). "From Friendship to Patronage: France-Israel Relations, 1958–1967," *Diplomacy & Statecraft*, 21:2, pp. 240–58.

Horne, Alistair (2006). *A Savage War of Peace: Algeria 1954–1962.* New York: NYRB Classics.

Jasse, Richard L. (1991). "The Baghdad Pact: Cold War or Colonialism?" *Middle Eastern Studies*, 27:1, pp. 140–56.

Kolodziej, Edward (1974). *French International Policy under de Gaulle and Pompidou: The Politics of Grandeur.* Ithaca, NY: Cornell University Press.

Kolodziej, Edward (1980). "France and the International Arms Trade," *International Affairs*, 56:1.

Kyle, Keith (2003). *Suez: Britain's End of Empire in the Middle East.* New York: I.B. Tauris.

Lacouture, Jean (1993). *De Gaulle: The Ruler, 1945–1970.* New York: W.W. Norton & Company.

Marlowe, John (1971). *Perfidious Albion: The Origins of Anglo-French Rivalry in the Levant.* London: Elek Books.

Ovendale, Ritchie (1994). "Great Britain and the Anglo-American Invasion of Jordan and Lebanon in 1958," *The International History Review*, 16:2, pp. 284–304.

Peyrefitte, Alain (2002). *C'était de Gaulle.* Paris: Gallimard.

Rabinovich, Abraham (1997). *The Boats of Cherbourg*. Annapolis MD: Naval Institute Press.

Rondot, Philippe (1987). "France and Palestine: From Charles de Gaulle to Francois Mitterrand," *Journal of Palestine Studies*, 16:3, pp. 87–100.

Shalom, Zaki (2008). "Israel's Foreign Minister Eban meets President de Gaulle and Prime Minister Wilson on the Eve of the Six Day War," *Israel Affairs*, 14:2, pp. 277–87.

Slonin, Shlomo (1987). "Origins of the 1950 Tripartite Declaration on the Middle East," *Middle Eastern Studies* 23:2, pp. 135–49.

Styan, David (2006). *France and Iraq: oil, arms and French policy-making in the Middle East*. New York: I.B. Tauris.

Vaïse, Maurice (1998). *La grandeur: Politique étrangère du général de Gaulle, 1958–1969*. Paris: Fayard.

Vaïse, Maurice (2009). *La Puissance ou l'influence? La France dans le monde depuis 1958*. Paris: Fayard.

NOTES

1. Charles de Gaulle, Press Conference at the Elysée Palace, 27 November 1967.

2. Raymond Aron (1968), *De Gaulle, Israël et les Juifs*, Paris: Plon.

3. The best known violation of the arms embargo happened when Israel hijacked five missiles boats that had been ordered before the war from the French harbour at Cherbourg in 1969. See: Abraham Rabinovich (1997), *The Boats of Cherbourg*, Annapolis: Naval Institute Press.

4. As Israel's ambassador to Paris, Walter Eytan remarked in 1967, de Gaulle's "motives were, and still remain unclear. His aides explained that he acted out of genuine concern for Israel, threatened by all the Arab states. But we can speculate as to other reasons as well, such as fear of a new global war, his desire to play the mediator, the fear that after the outbreak of the war no one would turn to France, but only the two giants, or even (and for this I have no proof whatsoever), caring for the fate of the Arab people which constitute a part of the 'Third World' that he has been courting for many years now." Walter Eytan, quoted in Gadi Heimann (2010a), In "Search of a Route to World Power: General de Gaulle, the Soviet Union, and Israel in the Middle Eastern Crisis of 1967", *The International History Review* 32:1, p. 69.

5. Raymond Aron (1968), Op. cit.; Edward Kolodziej (1974), *French International Policy under de Gaulle and Pompidou: The Politics of Grandeur*, Ithaca: Cornell University Press; Maurice Vaïse (2009), *La Puissance ou l'influence? La France dans le monde depuis 1958*, Paris: Fayard.

6. Gadi Heimann (2010a), Op. cit.

7. Michel Bar-Zohar (1986), *Histoire secrète de la guerre d'Israël*, Paris: Fayard.

8. Philippe Rondot (1987), "France and Palestine: From Charles de Gaulle to Francois Mitterrand", *Journal of Palestinian Studies* 16:3, pp. 87–100; Paul-Marie de la Gorce (1999), *De Gaulle*, Paris: Perrin.

9. Maurice Vaïsse has portrayed de Gaulle's shift as normalization. See: Maurice Vaïse (2009), Op. cit.; David Styan on the other hand has argued that it represented more of a reinvention than a return to a long-term trajectory. See: David Styan (2006), *France and Iraq: Oil, Arms and French Policy-Making in the Middle East*, New York: I.B. Tauris.

10. Maurice Vaïsse (2009), Op.cit., pp. 356–57.

11. Sylvia K. Crosbie (1974), *A Tacit Alliance: France and Israel from Suez to the Six Day War*, Princeton, N.J.: Princeton University Press, p. 50.

12. John Marlowe (1971), *Perfidious Albion: The Origins of Anglo-French Rivalry in the Levant*, London: Elek Books.

13. David Styan (2006), Op. cit., p. 33.

14. Shlomo Slonin (1987), "Origins of the 1950 Tripartite Declaration on the Middle East," *Middle Eastern Studies* 23:2, pp. 135–49

15. Richard L. Jasse (1991), "The Baghdad Pact: Cold War or Colonialism?" *Middle Eastern Studies*, 27:1, pp. 140–56.

16. Sylvia K. Crosbie (1974), Op. cit., p. 9.

17. Charles-Robert Ageron (1989), "L'Algérie, dernière chance de la puissance française: Étude d'une mythe politique (1954–1962)," *Relations Internationales*, 57, pp. 113–39.

18. On France during the Algerian crisis, see: Alistair Horne (2006), *A Savage War of Peace: Algeria 1954–1962*, New York: NYRB Classics.

19. On France's role in the Israeli nuclear programme, see: Avner Cohen (1998), *Israel and the Bomb*, New York: Columbia University Press.

20. On the arms contract, see: Sylvia K. Crosbie (1974), pp. 60–61.

21. On the Suez Crisis, see: Keith Kyle (2003), *Suez: Britain's End of Empire in the Middle East*, New York: I.B. Tauris.

22. Sylvia K. Crosbie (1974), Op. cit., p. 90.

23. In September 1956, Shimon Peres secured the agreement that Israel would receive a 24 megaton nuclear reactor from France. Heiman, Gadi (2010), "Diverging Goals: the French and Israeli Pursuit of the Bomb, 1958–1962," *Israel Studies*, 15:2, pp. 104–26.

24. Charles de Gaulle (1970), *Mémoires d'Espoir*, Paris: Plon, p. 277.

25. Ritchie Ovendale (1994), "Great Britain and the Anglo-American Invasion of Jordan and Lebanon in 1958," *The International History Review*, 16:2, pp. 284–304.

26. Apart from Israel, France at this stage was engaged in nuclear cooperation negotiations with West Germany and Italy on the possibility of building a joint isotope separation plant. Gadi Heiman (2010), Op. cit., p. 111.

27. Charles de Gaulle (1970), Op. cit., p. 266.

28. On this point see: Gadi Heiman (2010), Op. cit.; Avner Cohen (1998), Op. cit.

29. Raymond Aron (1968), Op. cit., p. xxvi.

30. On de Gaulle's meeting with Eshkol, see: Sylvia K. Corsbie (1974), p. 179.

31. Gadi Heimann (2010), "From Friendship to Patronage: France-Israel Relations, 1958–1967," *Diplomacy & Statecraft*, 21:2, pp. 240–258.

32. The Evian Accords put an end to the Algerian War, leading to a formal ceasefire on 19 March 1962. The Accords granted certain property and religious rights to

the French *colons* and permitted France to maintain its naval facilities at Mers-el-Kébir. In return France provided financial and technical assistance to the new Algerian government. See: Alistair Horne (2006), *A Savage War of Peace: Algeria 1954–1962*, New York: NYRB Classics.

33. Edward Kolodziej (1980), "France and the International Arms Trade," *International Affairs*, 56:1.

34. Vaïse, Maurice (1998), *La grandeur: Politique étrangère du général de Gaulle, 1958–1969*, Paris: Fayard, p. 452–500.

35. Edward Kolodziej (1974), Op. cit.

36. Sylvia K Crosbie (1974), Op. cit., pp. 24.

37. Gadi Heimann (2010b), Op. cit., pp. 252–53.

38. Ibid.

39. Sylvia K. Crosbie (1974), Op. cit., pp. 202–03.

40. Zaki Shalom (2008), "Israel's Foreign Minister Eban meets President de Gaulle and Prime Minister Wilson on the Eve of the Six Day War," *Israel Affairs*, 14:2, pp. 277–87

41. De Gaulle (1970), p. 266.

42. Sylvia K. Crosbie (1974), Op. cit., p. 191.

43. On that point, see: Gadi Heimann (2010a), Op. cit.

44. Walter Eytan cited in Zaki Shalom (2008), Op cit., p. 284.

45. Alain Peyrefitte (2002), *C'était de Gaulle*, Paris: Gallimard, p. 1492.

46. Gadi Heimann (2010a), Op. cit., pp. 83–84.

47. France concluded negotiations for arms deals with Iraq, Saudi Arabia and Kuwait in 1968, followed by a large contract for 110 Mirage fighter jets with Libya in 1969. See: David Styan (2006), Op. cit., pp. 112–13.

48. France opened negotiations for oil concession and joint exploration with Iraq in August 1967, followed by a similar agreement with Libya in April 1968. See: Nasser H. Aruri & Natalie Hevener (1969), "France and the Middle East, 1967–1968," *Middle East Journal*, 23:4, pp. 500–501.

49. David Styan (2006), Op. cit., p. 66.

50. See: Letter of Charles de Gaulle to David Ben Gurion from 30 December 1967, replicated in translation in the *New York Times* of 10 January 1968.

51. Gadi Heimann (2010a), Op. cit.

52. Jean Lacouture (1993), *De Gaulle: The Ruler, 1945–1970*, New York: W.W. Norton & Company.

Chapter 9

De Gaulle and American Power

Dana H. Allin

In the first volume of his memoirs, Henry Kissinger recounts the evening that French President Charles de Gaulle summoned him for a terse interview. As liquor was being served following an Elysee dinner for Kissinger's boss, President Nixon,

> an aide told me that the General wished to see me. Without the slightest attempt at small talk, de Gaulle greeted me with the query: "Why don't you get out of Vietnam?" "Because," I replied, "a sudden withdrawal might give us a credibility problem." "Where?" the General wanted to know. I mentioned the Middle East. "How very odd," said the General from a foot above me. "It is precisely in the Middle East that I thought your enemies had the credibility problem."[1]

Kissinger's anecdote is pregnant with what has been, arguably, the central cause of Franco-American—and, by partial extension, transatlantic—misunderstanding since World War II. That misunderstanding concerns the nature and role of power. De Gaulle's essential view was that America had more power than was good for it or good for the world, more than it sometimes understood and yet less than it often imagined. Such subtleties were not *always* lost on his American interlocutors—Kissinger himself a prime example of a U.S. official who professed to appreciate and admire de Gaulle's philosophy of power, even if its expression was gratuitously "wounding" to American sensibilities.[2] Of course, de Gaulle challenged America's power and global leadership during a decade, the 1960s, when its limits were becoming painfully obvious to everyone. Four decades later, French President Jacques Chirac criticized American pretensions to unipolar omnipotence at a time when Washington Groupthink was fairly

99

well sealed against the possibility that the United States was headed for a fall. Chirac's bad faith was simply assumed, just as de Gaulle's supposedly "anti-American" animus proved convenient for discounting his warnings about Vietnam. Yet given that Chirac's warnings on Iraq, like de Gaulle's on Vietnam, turned out to be not just prescient, but also objectively in the service of U.S. interests, it is worth looking back to their roots in a General's vision.

THE CONSERVATIVE CHALLENGE

The Gaullist challenge was confounding to American pretensions not least because it was an essentially conservative rebuke at a time when the United States was waging cold war on a left-right axis. Left-right distinctions, to be sure, did not always have strategic salience: America was pretty successful in promoting and aligning with European leftists in the form of anti-communist social democrats who, as often as not, were likely to castigate Washington for taking an insufficiently hard-line against Soviet encroachments and intimidation.[3] Still, it looked like a genuine left-right ideological struggle in much of Africa, Asia, and Latin America, where post-colonial, nationalist resistance to American hegemony and the American model of modernization was either explicitly aligned with Soviet interests or susceptible to Maoist, Trotskyite, or Castro-style ideologies to a degree that led Washington to discount any supposed independence from Moscow. Washington's embrace of a wide array of right-wing thugs and dictators was one unfortunate consequence of this discounting. In any event, the Americans could be forgiven for assuming that they had their right flank covered.

Yet here in de Gaulle was a coherent conservative critique of American power and hegemony. The Gaullist critique was not, moreover, *sui generis:* it found an echo in the conservative anxieties of de Gaulle's American contemporaries such as George F. Kennan and Robert A. Taft. De Gaulle, naturally, was not so preoccupied as these Americans with the American domestic political and constitutional damage that they feared would result from an American imperial mission. But like Kennan, he favored a multipolar balance of power–a system, in David P. Calleo's words, akin to "continental Europe's post-Napoleonic balance" instead of recreating "the worldwide *Pax Brittanica* that enchanted so many American analysts."[4] Like Kennan, de Gaulle was both appalled by the prospect of a world divided into Soviet and American spheres, and reasonably confident that the enduring force of fissiparous nationalism would render those blocs unsustainable.[5] As

President of France, the General did what he could to make the American bloc unmanageable.

Gaullism rubbed up first against American liberalism: the FDR administration and then, with de Gaulle's return to power, the Kennedy and Johnson Administrations. American liberals—as well as British Labor politicians–perceived an authoritarian and reactionary nationalism: in his disdain for party politics; in an absurd mysticism (once, during the war, as General Eisenhower's political adviser tried to discuss a point of French politics, de Gaulle interrupted him: "What you say may be true, but I've been in France for a thousand years"),[6] and, after the war, during the first phase of exile from power, in his strange political rallies, stage managed by Andre Malraux, with Nuremberg-style lighting and Mussolini-style thugs.[7] The irony regarding these early accusations, of course, was that de Gaulle would go on to save French democracy when he faced down a military coup by colonial officers appalled at his decision to grant Algerian independence. Even so, at a time when the Kennedy administration was pushing anti-Communist internationalism and European federalism, de Gaulle looked every bit the reactionary nationalist.

POWER AND BALANCE

American frustration with the Gaullist challenge reached crisis dimensions some thirty years after de Gaulle's death, with the transatlantic argument over the Bush administration's decision to invade Iraq. Three months after the start of that campaign, convinced, prematurely, of vindication, the administration set out one of its most elaborate critiques of the Gaullist idea in a speech by National Security Adviser Condoleezza Rice at the International Institute for Strategic Studies in London. French concepts of multi-polarity were not only misguided, Rice insisted, but profoundly dangerous:

[S]ome have spoken admiringly—almost nostalgically—of "multi-polarity," as if it were a good thing, to be desired for its own sake. The reality is that "multi-polarity" was never a unifying idea, or a vision. It was a necessary evil that sustained the absence of war but it did not promote the triumph of peace. Multi-polarity is a theory of rivalry; of competing interests—and at its worst—competing values. We have tried this before. It led to the Great War—which cascaded into the Good War, which gave way to the Cold War. Today this theory of rivalry threatens to divert us from meeting the great tasks before us. Why would anyone who shares the values of freedom seek to put a check on those values? Democratic institutions themselves are a check on the excesses of power. Why should we seek to divide our capacities for good, when they can be so much more effective united? Only the enemies of freedom would cheer this division.[8]

This was an extreme, albeit sharply cogent, expression of an enduring American assumption. With important exceptions such as Kennan and Kissinger, Americans have traditionally opposed "balance-of-power" diplomacy as something anachronistically and even wickedly European. Another way of putting it is that American leaders have generally lacked any notion of power itself as possessing an independent moral dimension. Power has been seen as good or bad depending only on whether good or bad people or states wielded it.

De Gaulle took a more classically tragic view. Balance of power was a moral imperative in itself, because the possessor of excessive power almost inevitably falls victim to hubris, losing touch with the reality of limits. Such was the downfall of dictators, de Gaulle wrote, it being "the destiny of all dictators to go too far in what they undertake,"[9] and it was likewise for unbridled nations. Hence, during World War II, his famous account of the

> messianic impulse [that] now swelled the American spirit and oriented it toward vast undertakings. The United States, delighting in her resources, feeling that she no longer had in herself sufficient scope for her energies, wishing to help those who were in misery or bondage the world over, yielded in her turn to that taste for interventions in which the instinct for domination cloaked itself.[10]

This messianic impulse was well reflected, de Gaulle observed, in President Roosevelt, whose "will to power cloaked . . . in idealism" could be forgiven, he implied, as it was "only human."[11]

The flip side of overweening power and ambition was excessive weakness, a preoccupation of de Gaulle from the Third Republic until his retirement from the presidency in 1969. This preoccupation was at the root of behavior that his American and British interlocutors so frequently interpreted as narrowly petty. The General, in Harold Macmillan's memorable phrase, was constantly returning to his sense of grievance, "like a dog to its vomit."[12] Yet de Gaulle's apparent pettiness was grounded in the philosophical conviction that deference and weakness can become bad habits. "For a great people to have the free disposition of itself and the means to struggle to preserve it is an absolute imperative," he declared in a famous press conference. For "if one spontaneously loses, even for a while, the free disposition of oneself, there is a strong risk of never regaining it."[13]

The Third Republic had been the General's first school of weakness. He had watched in dismay as a series of quarrelsome and unstable governments failed to come to grips with the predicament of the rising threat from Germany.[14] When the Third Republic fell, much of de Gaulle's attention turned to the primary goal of rehabilitating a subjective French self-confidence amidst objective conditions of near helplessness. Thus his endless insistence on France's *"rang"*-rank among its allies, who accused him of devoting more worry to the struggle against them than to the one against Hitler. Yet the logic of de Gaulle's position was in understanding that the French Resistance and Free French forces could contribute only marginally to defeating Germany in any event. Their other task, comparable in importance, was mythmaking in the service of French nationalism.[15] By extension, in de Gaulle's view, the actual weakness of the French position could not be acknowledged. When some of his Free French colleagues in London became embarrassed by his behavior toward their UK hosts, de Gaulle cabled this response: "Our greatness and our weakness lies solely in our inflexibility concerning the rights of France. We will need that inflexibility until we are on the far side of the Rhine."

The same inflexibility animated his actions, however, long after that river was crossed. Especially after returning to power in 1958, his policies were a catalogue of resistance to the logic of American hegemony. As part of a general Franco-German reconciliation, he sought to persuade West Germany's Adenauer to choose France as a favored ally over America; when the Bundestag sought to blur that choice by attaching a pro-American preamble to the 1963 Franco-German Treaty, de Gaulle lost interest. He vetoed Britain's application to join the European Common Market, calling the United Kingdom a stalking horse for the United States. He refused to join the "multilateral force," an American scheme for pooling French, British, and (some) U.S. nuclear forces. He resisted the U.S. flexible-response effort to coordinate and, hopefully, restrain a possible nuclear war, and in fact embraced, at least in part, a French nuclear doctrine that anticipated sabotaging flexible response. He flew to Canada to praise Québécois separatism; to South America, where he invoked Latin solidarity; and to Phnom Penh, where he denounced America's war in Vietnam. As American efforts to pay for that war started to put the dollar under strain, de Gaulle added to the pressure by suddenly demanding gold for France's dollar balances. He set a new course for French policy in the Middle East, courting favor with the Arabs and repudiating France's 1956 guarantee to stand by Israel if Egypt once more tried to close the Straits of Tiran. And of course, de Gaulle in 1966 withdrew France from NATO's military command, expelling American troops and bases. While reaffirming France's formal alliance with the United States, he added pointedly that should war come, France would *then* decide whether to participate.

ELEMENTS OF POWER: THE DOLLAR, NUCLEAR WEAPONS, NATIONALISM

Highly annoying as they were to Washington, these sometimes small-bore actions rested on two larger rationales. The first concerned the necessity for France to remain master of her own house, as free as possible from American hegemony. The second was de Gaulle's conviction that France could *afford* this freedom: the struggle against American hegemony would not deliver France over to Soviet hegemony because Moscow was not powerful enough to exercise that hegemony. These two rationales derived, in turn, from de Gaulle's understanding of the triangular relationship between the United States, Soviet Union, and France (or more broadly, Western Europe), which was configured through myriad elements of power. Of these elements, three were the subject of particular Gaullist insight: nuclear weapons, the dollar, and nationalism.

Nuclear weapons. Gaullist nuclear doctrine cast significant doubt on the reliability of American protection, but it also offered the hope for French national *self*-protection based on a multi-polar structure of nuclear deterrence. The French nuclear challenge had come as early as 1954 from a group of military writers spearheaded by General Pierre Gallois. In a series of journal articles Gallois joined the debate about whether France should develop her own nuclear force. Part of his contribution was a seminal critique of the logic of extended deterrence. In his classic book of 1961, translated in English as *The Balance of Terror,* he restated his argument from that earlier debate.

> Since the United States itself is vulnerable to Soviet ballistic missiles, the automatic nature of American intervention is less certain. If, therefore, America were to come to the support of a friendly nation, she would be placed in a difficult situation from a military point of view. She would either have to destroy her adversary's reprisal forces—and such an operation would be all the less feasible because these forces, long since alerted, would be protected by underground storage or mobility—or else suffer their terrible effects. To annihilate the Soviet cities would present no operational difficulties but would not paralyze the Soviet reprisal, which would be launched at once. Threatened with enormous damages if she were to come to the aid of Great Britain, America might hesitate. And once the likelihood of American intervention was in doubt, the U.S.S.R. would recover a share of its freedom of action with regard to the United Kingdom.

> It is, in fact, plausible for the potential aggressor to make the following calculation: if seriously threatened a powerful adversary would probably use his megatons of destruction in retaliation. But in a question of intervening for the sake of another country, even a friendly power, hesitation is particularly likely, for the laws of nuclear strategy are unfavorable to such intervention.[16]

The nuclear doctrine that Gallois and others consequently developed stressed that the credibility of nuclear deterrence depends on the value to the defender of what was being defended. Only when the most vital national interests were menaced could the threat to trigger nuclear war, and probable national suicide, seem plausible. The implications of this strategic view naturally served to undermine alliances in a nuclear age, a reality that Kissinger would later find most unsettling not so much regarding France, but because it was the stated rationale of one of West German Chancellor Willy Brandt's key advisers, Egon Bahr, for Brandt's *Ostpolitik.*[17] But the doctrine also held the promise of restoring some freedom of action to recently demoted world powers. Gallois' writings stressed the equalizing power that nuclear weapons confer on a smaller power, if that power makes clear its absolute determination to defend its sovereignty even at the risk of nuclear annihilation.

Starting with the Fourth Republic, taking on greater urgency under de Gaulle, France created its own nuclear force around the idea that Paris needed only a large enough force to inflict unacceptable damage on an aggressor's industrial and population centers, regardless of any superiority that the aggressor enjoyed. So long as the French force was survivable, a condition satisfied by the early 1970s when France launched nuclear-armed submarines, the effectiveness of her deterrent depended more on the perceived importance of what she was defending than on any quantitative military balance—or so de Gaulle himself claimed, in one of his characteristically pedagogical press conferences:

> once reaching a certain nuclear capability, and with regard to one's own direct defense, the proportion of respective means has no absolute value. Indeed, since a man and people can die only once, the deterrent exists provided that one has the means to wound the possible aggressor mortally, that one is determined to do it and that the aggressor is convinced of it.[18]

The dollar. What de Gaulle called the "inordinate privilege" of the U.S. dollar derived in large measure from the extraordinary burden that America assumed after 1945 in financing the world's—especially Europe's—post-war economic recovery, and in extending its military protection against Soviet threats. This was not pure altruism, of course, but the fact that economic recovery and strategic stability were manifestly in the American interest did not diminish the generosity of the U.S. post-war project, as de Gaulle himself recognized.

Yet the financial underpinnings of this project, which were established at Bretton Woods but survived Bretton Woods' demise, carried at least two significant long-term problems for the international system. First, the seigniorage accorded to the United States through the dollar's reserve-currency role allowed Washington to ignore fundamental strategic choices and limits. The power to print the world's currency conveyed the ability to finance a global strategic role without commensurately taxing American citizens. Arguably, the ongoing economic crisis stems from this American habit of ignoring limits: the basic mechanism for U.S. and Chinese growth for almost a generation—American over-consumption and Chinese over-saving—created the massive imbalances that helped cause the financial meltdown of 2008 and the consequent Great Recession.

Second, and with much earlier effect, the accumulation during the 1960s of large dollar balances in the reserves of West European countries constituted a kind of "imperial tax," in David Calleo's memorable phrase; enjoying U.S. military protection while their own defense budgets remained modest, thereby able to enjoy economic growth and to finance generous welfare states, these countries were reluctant to complain too loudly. Yet the dollar balances had inflationary consequences for countries, like France, where inflation was becoming an acute and endemic problem. For de Gaulle, taking tutelage from the economist Jacques Rueff, the whole system had become "abusive and dangerous."[19]

De Gaulle's answer was a return to the gold standard:

> We hold as necessary that international exchange be established . . . on an indisputable monetary base that does not carry the mark of any particular country. What base? In truth, one does not see how in this respect it can have any criterion, any standard, other than gold. Eh! Yes, gold, which does not change in nature, which is made indifferently into bars, ingots, and coins, which does not have any nationality, which is held eternally and universally. . . . No money counts . . . except in direct or indirect relation to gold. Doubtless, one does not think to impose on each country the manner in which it should conduct itself domestically. But the supreme law, the golden rule . . . that must be placed in operation and honored in international economic relations is the obligation to bring into equilibrium between monetary zones, through transfers of the precious metal, the balance of payments resulting from their exchanges.[20]

In truth, de Gaulle's remedy did not make much sense except as a metaphor for monetary stability. The virtues enumerated here by de Gaulle are also the vices of such a system if it were to be put back into practice. There is a limited amount of gold in the world, and its role in putting a brake on price rises would be savagely deflationary in a world of rising populations, aspirations and living standards. Even as a metaphor it could cause harm. Central bank fixation on price stability has clear benefits but also undeniable human costs.

Certainly the entrenched continental European philosophy of monetary conservatism has hardly offered a better answer to the current crisis than America's default Keynesianism. To be sure, Europeans have not faced as dire an employment collapse as have Americans. Still, the European conservatism fails to grasp the well-demonstrated lesson that a traumatic collapse of demand requires monetary loosening as well as government deficit spending to fill the void.

The Great Recession caused ongoing emergency conditions, however, requiring emergency—and, by definition, temporary—remedies. The long-term source of the emergency is correctly identified in the Gaullist critique, as Robert Skidelsky, a convinced Keynesian, recently acknowledged:

> The new [post—Bretton Woods] construction allowed the United States to continue to enjoy the political benefits of 'seigniorage'—the right to acquire real resources through the printing of money. The real resources the United States acquired were not just free consumer goods, but the ability to deploy large military forces overseas without having to tax its own citizens to do so. Every historian knows that a hegemonic currency is part of an imperial system of political relations. The Americans acquiesced in the unbalanced economic relations initiated by East Asian currency under-valuation because they ensured the persistence of unbalanced political relations. U.S. acceptance of a reform package aimed at ending global macro-economic imbalances thus depends on its willingness to accept a much more plural world–one in which other centers of power in Europe, China, Japan, Latin America, and the Middle East assume responsibility for their own security, and in which the rules of the game for a world order which can preserve the peace while effectively tackling the challenges posed by terrorism, climate change, and abuse of human rights, are negotiated, and not imposed.[21]

Meanwhile, the American disease of imagined omnipotence[22] has achieved its *reductio ad absurdum* in the contemporary Republican Party, which holds as non-negotiable the principle that taxes can only go down and never go up, without the whisper of an acknowledgement that this principle must constrain American strategic reach and ambition. (Nor, in truth, do the Republicans offer any significant proposals for cutting domestic spending.) De Gaulle certainly would recognize the disease; whether he would laugh or cry at this ultimate progression of it is an open question.

Nationalism. To identify nationalism as a third source of power may seem a bit of a stretch; yet his keen sense of nationalism was central to de Gaulle's ideas of power precisely because its enduring geopolitical force was something that the General perceived much more clearly than most of his American contemporaries. This perception suffused all of his ideas and policies regarding Franco-American relations.

De Gaulle accused Americans of stressing the unity of Western power because it justified U.S. hegemony. "In politics and in strategy, as in the economy," he said, "monopoly quite naturally appears to the person who holds it to be the best possible system."[23] Of course, his own devotion to divided leadership was also self-serving, as it justified a greater role for France. De Gaulle's ideology seemed opportunistic: He turned on the Anglo-Saxons only after trying to join their club, proposing to Eisenhower a three-power directorate to control the West's nuclear weapons. It was doubly irritating to Americans, moreover, that he played the game of independence while continuing to benefit from a happy fact of geography: West Germany, loaded down with U.S. troops and weapons, stood between France and the Red Army.

Opportunistic or not, however, de Gaulle's multi-polar vision was acute, insofar as it focused on the force of nationalism as a solvent of the Soviet bloc. "In 1958 I considered that the world situation was very different from what it had been at the time of the creation of NATO," he would later write, recalling the year of his return to power.

> It now seemed fairly unlikely that the Soviets would set out to conquer the West, at a time when all the Western nations were back on an even keel and making steady material progress. Communism, whether it rises from within or erupts from without, has little chance of taking root without the help of some national calamity. The Kremlin knows this very well.[24]

Placing "the totalitarian yoke" on 300 million West Europeans was an unlikely project, he added, "when it was difficult enough to hold down a third as many people" in Eastern Europe. Under conditions of even minimal nuclear deterrence, moreover, "What madness it would be," for Moscow to attempt a war of conquest.

De Gaulle's vision was acute because of, not in spite of, his nineteenth-century worldview. Where the more modern Americans saw ideologies, de Gaulle saw "eternal" nations and he assumed that national feeling would outlast Communism. Like Kennan, de Gaulle saw the Soviet Union as an old-style Russian empire, severely overstretched. East European nationalism would inevitably revive; the Soviets could repress it by force, as in Budapest in 1956, but that necessity would make the occupied dominions a long-term weakness rather than an asset.

And the Soviet Union faced a more immediate challenge from China, which was linked to Moscow only by the thin reed of ideology. Indeed, shared allegiance to communism fuelled their rivalry. Accusing each other of heresy, the ancient, nationalist jealousies of Asia's two major land powers re-emerged. De Gaulle's emphasis on nationalism made him appreciate sooner than most Americans (Kennan again being a notable exception) the geopolitical significance of Sino-Soviet rivalry.

CONSEQUENCES?

Did de Gaulle's ideas about American power have real-world impact on the exercise of it? The reasonable answer is that the consequences were limited but significant. The emergence of Gaullist doctrine on nuclear weapons certainly came at a neuralgic moment in America's own thinking on the matter. Immediately upon assuming office, President Kennedy was appalled by the realization that the United States had no capacity to defend its interests in Berlin except through nuclear war, which he considered likely to become an apocalyptic spasm killing tens of millions. This was not an abstract fear; Khrushchev, coping with his own Berlin crisis,[25] was threatening to conclude a separate peace with East Germany that would end allied rights in West Berlin and, as the Americans saw it, seriously damage the credibility of America's security guarantee for all of Western Europe.[26] Rattled by Khrushchev's bluster, Kennedy, upon recovering his nerve, determined to increase U.S. conventional capabilities and also directed his Defense Secretary, Robert McNamara, to formulate a more rational strategy for using nuclear weapons. The result, "flexible response," a concept for graduated and controlled escalation, inevitably was more reassuring to distant Americans than to Europeans on whose territory this escalation would take place. The implications of Gaullist doctrine, on the other hand, were directly at odds with the American effort to control the risk and damage of nuclear war. The Gaullist justification, of course, was that the Americans were deluded to imagine controlled and limited nuclear exchanges: the greater uncertainty introduced by "multiple" centers of nuclear decision-making was a better guarantee of conventional as well as nuclear deterrence. Thankfully, these Franco-American tensions and debates became increasingly hypothetical as the real threat of U.S.-Soviet nuclear war, or even conventional conflict in Europe, receded. To be sure, another Kennedy preoccupation of the early 1960s, nuclear proliferation, had returned with a vengeance by 2010, and the small nuclear arsenals of American allies—France, Britain and Israel—will be a complicating factor in solving the problem. Overall, however, America was able in the end to come to terms with the French nuclear program and its Gaullist rationale rather well.

On dollar diplomacy, de Gaulle's criticisms were directed at a system that was falling apart anyway. Most remarkable, perhaps, is that the pre-eminence of the dollar, with attendant privileges for the power that prints it, has continued long after the Bretton Woods fixed exchange-rate system was abandoned. European countries who felt exposed to America's exports of inflation when the dollar rate was fixed felt comparable pain over subsequent gyrations of the dollar's value after it floated, which affected not only trade competitiveness with the United States but intra-European exchange rates. Yet however much they might grumble, there was during the Cold War an enduring reason for European leaders to accept the situation, a reason that David Calleo has been eloquent in describing:

Throughout the Cold War, America's ability to create credit for itself in this fashion depended on two conditions: First, there was no real substitute for the dollar as a reserve currency. And second, the principal accumulators of exported dollars were Germany and Japan, U.S. military protectorates who absorbed their dollars as a kind of imperial tax. All things considered, the costs of accumulating the exported dollars was a cheap price for America's protection, and awkward to refuse. The United States was spending more on Europe's defense than the Europeans themselves.[27]

After the Cold War ended, however, Europe's leaders were freer to construct a system that afforded greater protection from the dollar. This benignly anti-American aspect of European monetary union was just one of several motivators for an audacious project at the heart of European Union. It has been hugely successful in many respects, but the flaw that economist critics identified from the outset—the mismatch between a single monetary policy and individual fiscal policies—has been painfully confirmed in the current financial and economic crisis. The future of the euro is, at the time of this writing, uncertain. If and when it recovers from the crisis, however, it is likely to be a force affecting America's ability to finance endless deficits.

Nationalism is a vaguer element of power, of course. In the Gaullist worldview, its greatest importance was that de Gaulle's perception of it was key to his understanding that Soviet control over the Warsaw Pact, not to mention Moscow's Chinese ally, was likely to be temporary. At the time, however, in relations between de Gaulle and the United States, it was the General's nationalist approach of French independence that was most vexing to America's leadership. It is worth pausing to consider, however, just *how* vexing it really was. De Gaulle's resistance to the Kennedy administration's federalist visions of European integration, his veto of UK membership in the Common Market, and his withdrawal of France from NATO's integrated command were all frustrating to U.S. policy-makers. Yet the American Presidents who were contemporaries of de Gaulle made it a point to tolerate him in the name of the broader Cold War struggle. It was only after de Gaulle left the scene, when the stakes, ironically, were smaller (because the existential U.S.-Soviet confrontation relaxed and then faded away), that Washington started to find Gaullist concepts of national independence to be truly intolerable.

John F. Kennedy had considerable respect for the French President, famously memorized passages of de Gaulle's memoirs to quote back to him on a state visit to Paris, and urgently wanted, according to Charles Bohlen and Ted Sorenson, "to figure out what made him [de Gaulle] tick."[28] As exasperating as Kennedy's aides generally found the French president, JFK also appeared to take de Gaulle's warnings about Vietnam to heart. Balking several times at advice that he introduce U.S. ground troops, Kennedy thought it worth noting that de Gaulle (in MacGeorge Bundy's paraphrase) "out of painful French experience, had spoken with feeling of the difficulty of fighting in this part of the world."[29]

We can only speculate on whether Kennedy, had he not been shot down, would have maintained this restraint on Vietnam and other matters. Lyndon B. Johnson, as he did order successive stages of escalation, seems to have consciously decided to insulate the controversy of America's Vietnam war from the question of mutual solidarity with allies in Europe.[30] This allowed important European leaders, including West Germany's Willy Brandt and the UK's Harold Wilson, to distance themselves from America's war in the face of rising popular opposition without their Atlanticist loyalties being questioned. Yet even by this standard, de Gaulle seemed to enjoy considerable indulgence from the White House. As George Ball, then Under Secretary of State (and, as it happens, another critic of the war), recalled: "[President Johnson] incessantly restrained me from making critical comments, even though he would never have taken the General's constant needling from any other foreign leader."[31] Ball was among the many administration officials urging a strong U.S. reaction to de Gaulle's decision to withdraw from NATO's integrated command, kicking the headquarters and U.S. troops out of France, but Johnson himself took a famously measured view: "When a man asks you to leave his house, you don't argue; you get your hat and go." [32]

The Gaullist legacy was somehow a more bitter pill for Washington to swallow.[33] On this score, Henry Kissinger presents a notably paradoxical player. Before joining the Nixon administration, Kissinger admonished the previous Democratic administrations for their unhappiness with Gaullist independence. A "united Europe," Kissinger wrote, "is likely to insist on a specifically European view of world affairs—which is another way of saying it will challenge American hegemony in Atlantic policy."[34] Later he wrote that the United States "could not expect to perpetuate the accident of Europe's postwar exhaustion into a permanent pattern of international relations."[35] And at the beginning of Nixon's first term, Kissinger urged a willing president to be more open than his predecessors to the French president's ideas.[36]

Yet whereas the Kennedy and Johnson administrations had a lot of problems with Gaullism in theory but accommodated themselves to it in practice, for the Nixon administration it was the opposite. This was probably related to the *Götterdämmerung* aspects of the administration's demise in 1973–74. With the President battling Watergate, Kissinger as Secretary of State had unusual scope to direct U.S. foreign policy. He became incensed, during and after the October 1973 Arab-Israeli war, at what he regarded as a French-led "stampede of disassociation" from U.S. efforts to manage the crisis. This

European reaction, spearheaded by French Foreign Minister Michel Jobert, coming soon after de Gaulle's death, was very much in the spirit of Gaullism. De Gaulle had decided to end France's tight alignment with Israel. Jobert now asked, of the Egyptian and Syrian armies attacking on two fronts: "Is the attempt to put one's foot back into one's own house necessarily a surprising act of aggression?"[37] Despite his own sympathy for the position of Egypt's president Anwar Sadat, the French policy was too much for Kissinger, who later argued that in an "emergency," allies "have an obligation to subordinate their differences to the realization that the humiliation of the ally who, for better or worse, is *most* strategically placed to affect the outcome weakens the structure of common defense and the achievement of joint purposes."[38] The Gaullist alternative, in Kissinger's now far-less-tolerant view, demonstrated the readiness to choose "among varieties of appeasement."[39]

Notwithstanding Kissinger's original good intentions, 1973 was arguably the low point in Franco-American Cold War relations. Within ten years, however, there emerged a surprising strategic affinity between the Fifth Republic's first Socialist government, under Francois Mitterrand, and the administration of Ronald Reagan, icon of Cold War conservatism. This affinity, which entailed a broad range of anti-Soviet coordination, was symbolized most vividly by Mitterrand's decision to stand before the *Bundestag* to urge German deployment of American Pershing II's and ground-launched cruise missiles.[40] Some future tensions with Washington were stored up, however, by a different kind of Socialist departure from Gaullist principles. With German reunification and the end of the Cold War, the Mitterrand government abandoned most of de Gaulle's ambivalence about European integration. Though still far from being federalist in scope, this project of European Union started to raise worries in Washington about Europe as a serious geopolitical rival. The American anxieties were sufficient to inspire a somewhat notorious draft Pentagon document from the first Bush administration, arguing that it was in America's interest to prevent the emergence of any rival superpower.[41] Though the Clinton administration was generally more open to European ideas and models, it too was neuralgic about any putative European defense structure that implied real autonomy from NATO. And it was, of course, during the Clinton administration, that French Foreign Minister Hubert Vedrine expressed France's own concern about America's post-Cold War growth to "hyper-power" dimensions.[42] Yet all of this sniping remained at the level of theories about international relations, and against a base line of reasonably good transatlantic relations. This changed with the second Bush administration and the Iraq war of 2003, which turned the abstract arguments about uni-polar versus multi-polar international power structures into a life and death reality.

"Why would anyone who shares the values of freedom seek to put a check on those values?" asked Condoleezza Rice in her above-quoted speech of June 2003 at the IISS in London. She got her answer soon enough, in the carnage that civil war was to visit upon Iraq, and the huge losses in reputation and strategic resources suffered by the United States. The simple answer was that even "good" powers need to be balanced; even the avatar of freedom requires some restraint. American self-restraint was supposed to be built into its constitutional system. Checks and balances were built in by a group of founding drafters who were worried probably more than anything else about the national accumulation of executive power in wartime, and how this would threaten the new American democracy. As it happens, during the Second World War and then the Cold War, for good reasons and bad, these domestic checks and balances on executive power were very significantly eroded. But there was another, more amorphous system of checks and balances the American executive branch itself had built up—the post-Second World War system of alliances and international institutions. As Calleo, G. John Ikenberry and others have argued, these became an organic part of the American constitutional system.[43]

Any system of constitutional restraint—even an amorphous, organic and inchoate international system—requires not just rules but independent centers of power to enforce those rules. "Multi-polarity," a word to describe such independent centers of power, started to disappear from the French diplomatic vocabulary after 2003 as the Chirac government decided it was time to repair relations with Washington. This may have been a wise renunciation of an unnecessary semantic quarrel. To renounce Charles de Gaulle's insights on international power and the necessity of its balance, however, would be unwise in the extreme.

NOTES

1. Henry Kissinger, *White House Years* (Boston: Little, Brown, 1979), pp. 109–10.

2. Ibid.

3. After the Berlin Wall went up in 1961, for example, Berlin mayor Willy Brandt wrote to Kennedy, "Inaction or merely defensive action could provoke a crisis of confidence in the Western powers." Later, Brandt summarized the episode acidly: "The Soviet Union had defied the major power in the Western world and effectively humiliated it." See Dana H. Allin, *Cold War Illusions: America, Europe and Soviet Power, 1969–1989* (New York: St. Martin's, 1997) p. 20.

4. David P. Calleo, *Beyond American Hegemony: the Future of the Western Alliance.* (New York: Perseus, 1989), p. 33.

5. "I was a Gaullist before de Gaulle," said Kennan on himself; see John Lamberton Harper, *American Visions of Europe: Franklin D. Roosevelt, George F. Kennan, and Dean Acheson* (Cambridge: Cambridge University Press, 1994), p. 337.

6. Richard J. Barnet, *The Alliance—America, Europe, Japan: Makers of the Post War World* (New York: Simon and Schuster, 1983), p. 21.

7. Brian Crozier, *De Gaulle* (New York: Scribners, 1973), pp. 419–27.

8. Remarks by Dr. Condoleezza Rice, Assistant to the President for National Security Affairs, at the International Institute for Strategic Studies, London, 26 June 2003, www.iiss.org/recent-key-addresses/condoleezza-rice-address/.

9. De Gaulle, cited in David P. Calleo, *Europe's Future: The Grand Alternatives* (New York: Horizon Press, 1965), p. 117.

10. Charles de Gaulle, *The Complete War Memoirs of Charles de Gaulle, 1940–46, Vol. 2: Unity* (New York: Simon & Schuster 1964) pp. 573–74.

11. Ibid.

12. MacMillan, cited in Peter Mangold, *The Almost Impossible Ally: Harold Macmillan and Charles De Gaulle* (London: I.B. Tauris, 2006), p. 166.

13. De Gaulle press conference, January 14, 1963, *Major Addresses, Statements and Press Conferences of General Charles de Gaulle, May 19, 1958–January 31, 1964* (New York: French Embassy Press and Information Division, 1964), p. 216.

14. Charles de Gaulle, *The Complete War Memoirs of Charles de Gaulle*, Vol. I: *The Call to Honor 1940–1942* (New York: Simon and Schuster, 1964), chapters 1, 2.

15. This is not to endorse, in any form or fashion, certain Anglo-American libels against the real courage and sacrifice of French forces fighting the Germans at every stage of World War II. See Simon Serfaty, "Terms of Estrangement: The Unavoidable Franco-American Alliance," *Survival: Global Politics and Strategy*, Vol. 47, No. 3 (Autumn 2005). Responding to historian Niall Ferguson's claim that, "the French went down with scarcely a fight: mortality amounted to less than 1 per cent of the pre-war population," Serfaty notes that the May 1940 German offensive alone left over 100,000 French citizens dead, and nearly 200,000 wounded. These losses, he believes, amount to more than "scarcely a fight."

16. Pierre Gallois, *The Balance of Terror: Strategy for the Nuclear Age* (Boston: Houghton Mifflin, 1961), pp. 139–40.

17. "There [was] now a strategic balance and that meant that America would think twice before risking its own existence. Would America answer with nuclear missiles if the Russians took Hamburg? The answer [was] no. So détente was our only option." Egon Bahr, interview with author, Bonn, September 29, 1994. See Dana H. Allin, *Cold War Illusions: America, Europe and Soviet Power, 1969-1989* (New York: St. Martin's, 1997), pp. 38–40.

18. De Gaulle press conference, July 23, 1964, Ambassade de France, *Major Addresses, Statements and Press Conferences of General Charles de Gaulle* (New York: Service de presse et d'information, 1967), p. 25.

19. Christopher S. Chivvis, "Charles de Gaulle, Jacques Rueff and French International Monetary Policy under Bretton Woods," *Journal of Contemporary History*, Vol. 41, No. 4 (October 2006).

20. Charles de Gaulle, *Discours et Messages IV* (Paris: Pion, 1971), p. 333, as cited in Edward A. Kolodzieg, "French Monetary Diplomacy in the Sixties: Background Notes to the Current Monetary Crisis," *World Affairs*, Vol. 135, No. 1 (Summer 1972), p. 14.

21. Robert Skidelsky, "Notes on The Economic Crisis and the International Order," IISS Global Strategic Review, Geneva, 14 September 2009; www.iiss. org/conferences/global-strategic-review/global-strategic-review-2009/plenary -sessions-and-speeches-2009/lord-robert-skidelsky/.

22. For a masterful diagnosis, see David P. Calleo, *Follies of Power: America's Unipolar Fantasy* (Cambridge: Cambridge University Press, 2009).

23. De Gaulle press conference, January 14, 1963, *Major Addresses, Statements and Press Conferences of General Charles de Gaulle, May 19, 1958–January 31, 1964* (New York: French Embassy Press and Information Division, 1964), p. 217.

24. Charles de Gaulle, *Memoirs of Hope* (London: Weidenfield & Nicolson, 1971), pp. 200–01.

25. Khrushchev's crisis stemmed from the presence of a Western half-city deep in East Germany that allowed thousands of Germans to simply walk out on the supposed show-place of communist Europe.

26. The profound anxieties engendered by successive Berlin crises are masterfully conveyed in Richard Reeves, *President Kennedy: Profile of Power* (New York: Simon & Schuster, 1993).

27. David P. Calleo, "Obama's Dilemma: Enraged Opponents or Disappointed Followers," http://bcjournal.org/wp-content/uploads/2010/05/calleo-from-bcjia-mag_ final-2.pdf, p. 7.

28. "De Gaulle and Three Presidents," *Life Magazine,* 20 November 1970.

29. Gordon M. Goldstein, *Lessons in Disaster: McGeorge Bundy and the Path to War in Vietnam* (New York: Henry Holt, 2008), p. 56; see also, Lawrence J. Bassett and Stephen E. Pelz, "The Failed Search for Victory: Vietnam and the Politics of War," in ed. Thomas G. Paterson, *Kennedy's Quest for Victory: American Foreign Policy, 1961–1963* (New York: Oxford University Press, 1989), p. 229.

30. Thomas Allen Schwartz, *Lyndon Johnson and Europe: In the Shadow of Vietnam* (Cambridge: Harvard University Press, 2003).

31. George W. Ball, *The Past Has Another Pattern: Memoirs* (New York: W. W. Norton and Company, 1983), p. 336.

32. Thomas Allen Schwartz, *Lyndon Johnson and Europe,* op. cit., p. 145.

33. On the question of how "Gaullist" the General's successors really were, see Philip H. Gordon, *A Certain Idea of France: French Security Policy and the Gaullist Legacy* (Princeton, N.J.: Princeton University Press, 1993).

34. Henry Kissinger, *The Troubled Partnership: A Re-appraisal of the Atlantic Alliance* (New York: McGraw-Hill, 1965), p. 40.

35. Henry Kissinger, "Central Issues of American Foreign Policy," in Kermit Gordon, ed. *Agenda for the Nation* (Washington D.C.: Brookings Institution, 1968), p. 595.

36. Kissinger, *White House Years*, op. cit., pp. 104–11.

37. Alfred Grosser, *The Western Alliance: European-American Relations Since 1945* (New York: Vintage Books, 1982), p. 274.

38. Henry Kissinger, *Years of Upheaval* (Boston: Little, Brown & Co., 1982), p. 708.

39. Ibid, pp. 897–98.

40. Allin, *Cold War Illusions*, op.cit., p. 99.

41. "Lone Superpower Plan: Ammunition for Critics," *New York Times*, 10 March 1992.

42. "To Paris, US Looks Like a 'Hyperpower,'" *New York Times*, 5 February 1999, www.nytimes.com/1999/02/05/news/05iht-france.t_0.html.

43. David P. Calleo, *Follies of Power*, op. cit.; G. John Ikenberry, *After Victory: Institutions, Strategic Restraint and the Rebuilding of Order after Major Wars* (Princeton, N.J.: Princeton University Press, 2001).

Index

About the Contributors

Dana Allin is a senior fellow for U.S. Foreign Policy and Transatlantic Affairs and editor of *Survival* at the International Institute for Strategic Studies, London, and adjunct professor at the SAIS Bologna Center.

Timo Behr is research fellow for European foreign and security policy, Finnish Institute of International Affairs, Helsinki.

David P. Calleo is a university professor, Dean Acheson Professor, and director of European studies at SAIS, Washington.

Christopher S. Chivvis is a fellow at the Rand Corporation, Washington, and adjunct professor at SAIS, Washington.

John L. Harper is professor of American foreign policy and European studies at the SAIS Bologna Center.

Thomas Row is chair of history at the Diplomatic Academy, Vienna, and adjunct professor at the SAIS Bologna Center.

Benjamin M. Rowland is a former investment banker, World Bank staff member and a consultant on private sector policies for emerging market governments.

Michael Stuermer is professor emeritus of medieval and modern history at Friedrich-Alexander University, Erlangen-Nurnberg, and adjunct professor at the SAIS Bologna Center.

Lanxin Xiang is professor of international history and politics at The Graduate Institute of International Studies, Geneva.

CPSIA information can be obtained at www.ICGtesting.com
Printed in the USA
269944BV00003B/4/P